THE Fresh Flower
ARRANGER'S BIBLE

THE
Fresh Flower
ARRANGER'S BIBLE

❀

PAMELA WESTLAND

H
HERMES
HOUSE

This edition published by Hermes House
an imprint of
Anness Publishing Limited
Hermes House
88-89 Blackfriars Road
London SE1 8HA

A CIP catalogue record for this book is available from the British Library

Publisher: Joanna Lorenz
Project Editors: Judith Simons and Lindsay Porter
Photographer: Nelson Hargreaves
Designer: Tony Paine

Previously published as *The Essential Flower Arranger*

© Anness Publishing Limited 1994, 2000

1 3 5 7 9 10 8 6 4 2

CONTENTS

THE ESSENTIAL FLOWER ARRANGER

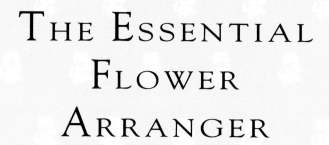

~

Whether you choose to arrange an armful of goldenrod
and marigolds in a painted jug or a subtle harmony of
freesias and lilies in a traditional urn, every flower
arrangement you compose can be an expression of your
own artistic style. The following pages will help you
develop that style, from the moment you gather a bunch
of flowers, through the choice of container and the
appropriate holding materials, to the overall shape of
the design and the most flattering way to display it.
It also takes an appreciative look at the relationship of
plant colours and textures and explains how you can
blend them to create the most pleasing effects, and
shows you step-by-step how to achieve both classic
arrangements and more informal compositions.

A bunch of yellow daffodils bringing a welcome ray of sunshine-brightness to the breakfast table on an early spring morning; a clutch of delicate wayside flowers gathered on a summer's day; a blaze of golden, red, russet, and brown flowers and fruits, the glories of autumn; a simple jug of glowing berries and glistening evergreen leaves, the pride of winter evoking thoughts of cosy log fires and frost on the windowpanes. However they are displayed, flowers and leaves can enhance the home throughout the year.

The way flowers and foliage are arranged, either together or separately, speaks volumes about individual style, personality, and even the mood of the moment. Give ten people an identical bunch of flowers, an identical container, an option of various types of stem-holding material, and a free hand to create the arrangement of their choice, and the results would be as varied and individual as the people themselves.

One arranger may delight in placing the flowers unceremoniously in the container to give them a carefree, just-as-they-were-picked look. Another, thinking perhaps of a niche or alcove as a suitable background, may form the flowers into a gracious curve, a design with a look of classic elegance, while a third may opt for the clean, uncluttered lines of a geometric shape such as a triangle. If one of the arrangers is feeling on top of the world at the time, he or she may create an exuberant sunburst of a design, whereas someone in a tranquil and reflective mood may unwittingly express those feelings in a design that takes a compact form and suggests restraint.

Two points arise from this imaginary experiment. Firstly, a flower design should be a free expression of the arranger's individual style, just as a painting should express the way an artist sees a subject. No design is 'wrong', though some arrangements may have a better sense of balance than others – a sense that is reassuringly easy to learn and achieve.

Secondly – and this is what makes flower arranging such an infinitely absorbing pastime – with that single bunch of flowers and that one specified container it should be possible to create any number of widely different designs, from country style to classic, to suit a variety of different backgrounds, situations, and occasions.

A MATTER OF STYLE

The choice of flower-arranging style, whether Oriental or traditional, elegant or romantic, is as personal as a sense of fashion, and just as rewarding to achieve. Your own instinctive style, the one that comes most readily to mind as soon as you start to put together your combination of containers, flowers, and foliage, will be influenced by your preference for colours, your normal life-style, and by the furnishings in your home. An impressive display of

An armful of spring flowers gathered straight from the garden might look like this. The design is etched with slender twigs laden with catkins. Visual weight at the base is provided by clusters of deep green ivy thick with berries. **Right**

Welcome guests with a floral arrangement on the steps or in the porch, or brighten a patio or balcony corner with a duet of garden flowers. The striped pottery container is filled with heavy and sweetly-scented bunches of white lilac and contrastingly delicate stems of deep mauve crane's-bill geranium. **Opposite**

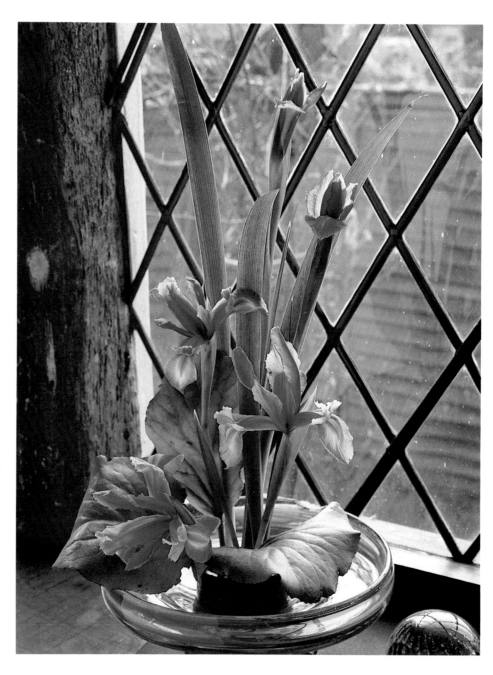

The heavy green glass dish suggests an arrangement of waterside plants in cool colours. With the simplicity of Oriental designs, the irises and hosta – or plantain lily – leaves compose a vertical outline. The speckled glass sphere adds to the feeling of cool, clear water. **Right**

snow-white lilies and expensive roses might look somewhat out of place if you were inviting friends to an informal supper in the kitchen, whereas a group of earthenware flowerpots or decorative preserve jars topped by single mopheads of greeny-blue hydrangeas could look both interesting and arresting.

When you plan to decorate your home for a special party or decorate a church or public hall for a wedding, you will still bring your own sense of style to the occasion, adapting your preferred designs to suit the degree of

formality. If, for example, baskets brimming over with garden flowers and trailing leaves are absolutely 'you', then you can still create designs in that genre for the special day. A wide, shallow basket cascading with pastel-coloured or all-white flowers would look as delightful as any more formal arrangement on top of a pedestal in church; and a deep basket filled to the brim with zingy, vibrant blooms would be a welcoming focal point at your party, whether in the porch, the hall, the hearth, or a corner of a room.

In fact, a flower arrangement can be the focal point of any room at any time, and one which you can change at whim, particularly when you are using fresh flowers. Just by your choice of flower colour, shape, and texture, you can create the kind of highlight in your room that makes visitors exclaim and think you have completely changed the decorations. In a room principally furnished with green and white, for example, you can 'keep it cool' and create an arrangement of ice-cold lilies, cream roses, and the glossiest of deep green leaves; a study of understatement. During a more flamboyant mood you could fill a similar container – a tall, cylindrical vase spatter-painted grey and white – with a medley of orange, yellow, and pink tulips, and suddenly the flowers would light up the entire room.

Once you realize the design potential of the simplest of arrangements, you will discover the everyday world around us is full of inspiration, a powerhouse of ideas that are there to be noticed – ideas for the mix and match of colours, for the juxtaposition of contrasting textures, and for varying styles of arrangement.

It is natural, perhaps, to turn first to the great artists for inspiration in matters of both colour and style. While no one expects you slavishly to copy a medieval or modernist painting, an art gallery or even a comprehensive selection of postcards or greetings cards in a shop can not only spark off ideas, but help you to assess and develop your own floral art style.

Among the works of the Old Masters you might, with your own home in mind, care to compare the tranquil simplicity of a white bowl of arching, wax-like tulips – a graceful focal point in a largely black-and-white room scheme – with the exuberance of an urn filled to profusion with tall and slender, round and robust flowers of every shape, texture, and hue, with gleaming fruit and vegetables for good measure and – a characteristically pastoral accessory – often a bird's nest as well. A similar generosity of both flower type and colour was revived in Victorian times, and paintings of that period provide just the edge of encouragement some flower arrangers may need to experiment with garden or hothouse floral blends of predominantly pink, purple, red, and blue flowers, with roses and camellias taking pride of place.

And then there are the Impressionists, whose style is both exciting and exhilarating to recreate with flowers in the home. You may choose to set a bunch of tissue-paper-thin poppies in the palest palette of pastel colours, soft pink, creamy-white, and the barest yellow, against the

Arranged in glorious profusion in a brown glazed pot, the spring flowers compose an all-round design with more than a hint of the early Dutch style.
Below

shafts of sunlight streaking in from a window; or a large bunch of petally marigolds in almost a single plane, the flowers nestling among bright sprays of goldenrod or delicate willow leaves.

A walk in the countryside, along the coast, or in the garden can be a rewarding primary source of inspiration to flower arrangers, just as it is to artists. The way the light glances through the trees may highlight a bunch of yellowing leaves, a clutch of berries, or a handful of seedheads, and alert you to the fact that nature has much to offer, even as winter approaches. The 'Wild Look'

A basket of autumn flowers, fruits, and seedheads makes a beautiful, if transient, decoration, and looks ahead to winter arrangements with its combination of fluffy old man's beard seedheads, glossy rosehips, russety spray chrysanthemums, sedum, and Chinese lanterns (winter cherry). **Left**

arrangement, composed of materials gathered in the wild at just such a time of year and inspired by the exaggerated curve of a couple of green-going-on-yellow oak branches, was derived in that very way.

It is not only the colour, but the texture of plant materials that plays a predominant part in how a floral display is perceived. The autumnal basket display mentioned above takes a leaf from nature's book and sets shiny-bright berries, which represent only a minimal proportion of the design as a whole, against matt textures and spiky outlines. The prominence of the berries has been assured because they are surrounded, as they may be in the wild, by the distinctly no-gloss element of old man's beard (*Clematis vitalba, C. virginiana*), the almost woody appearance of poppy seedheads, and the spiky spires of wheat.

Late in the season, a rose bush in the wild or in the garden creates a contrast of textures which can bring vibrant visual rewards indoors. As the rosehips ripen and glisten around it, a single rose, evocatively perceived as the last rose of summer, seems all the more romantic and delicate by comparison, and, in their turn, the berries seem even brighter and glossier.

This juxtaposition of shiny and matt, sparkling and velvety textures can be carried out to rewarding effect in floral displays of all kinds. Create the illusion of sidelighting, of sun shafts or lamplight, in a simple way by arranging glossy-petalled flowers such as lilies on one side of a container, and matt ones, maybe spider chrysanthemums, on the other. In a dark corner of a room, you can create the illusion of more light than there is by choosing the sunniest flowers and foliage available.

To create the impression of greater depth in an arrangement and impart a three-dimensional effect, position matt materials towards the back and into the centre, where they will be seen in partial shadow, and allow the shiny ones to come forward and steal the limelight.

In a garden or the countryside, you might notice the made-for-each-other pairing of glossy ivy leaves or wild roses entwined around the craggy bark of a tree, or on a seashore, the heightened beauty of delicate wild lupins (lupines) outlined against a breakwater. In this way, country and seashore walks can become treasure hunts: pieces of craggy wood are among the most precious *objets trouvés*, the craggier and more lichen-covered or salt-washed the better. Failing a lucky find of a piece of fallen tree or shapely driftwood, you can buy interesting specimens in florists' shops.

An angular piece of vinewood can become the 'tree' under which a drift of pale daffodils is arranged amid a mossy ground cover – an unusual interpretation of an Easter arrangement for a church. A sinuous piece of gnarled wood can simulate a fallen log and become a perfect foil, by virtue of the textural contrast, to clutches of delicate flowers; while knobbly twigs snapped off or fallen from an apple tree can create striking outlines and a natural look in otherwise conventional designs.

SHADES AND HUES

If on the spur of the moment you treat yourself to a few bunches of flowers from a market stall, or pause to admire a flower-filled garden, you will most certainly be influenced by colour, by the powerful impact of buckets of flowers spilling onto the pavement, or by the more considered effect of a formally maintained garden.

Setting aside the occasional impulse purchase, your choice of flowers for the home will usually take into

An uncluttered look for a kitchen, a study in cool greens and creams. The double narcissus are arranged with sprays of mimosa in bud and variegated ivy in an oval basket-weave container. **Above**

The warm glow of winter is exemplified by this gleaming leaf and berry arrangement in an old beer stein. The holly and ivy leaves look even more glossy when they are contrasted with matt foliage, in this case cypress and furry-leaved ballota. **Left**

Accessories can form a key element in still-life groups or even, as here, inspire the composition of the arrangement. The flowering currant, echoing the pattern of the potpourri cushion, forms an irregular triangle with bi-coloured tulips. **Right**

CHOOSING HUES

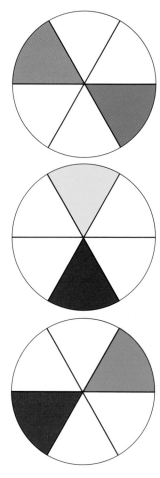

account your furnishings, the background against which they will be seen, and the effect you wish to create. A bunch of golden-yellow flowers, high on the list of impulse buys since yellow is considered a 'happy' colour, can work wonders in brightening a dull day. But, perhaps surprisingly, it is not just the colour of the flowers themselves that creates a vibrant and vigorous or calm and composed effect, but the interplay of flower and background colour together.

That bunch of sunshine-yellow daffodils, with all its cheering propensities, would have a limited impact in design terms if placed against an orange curtain or a window framing an expanse of green lawn. Move it to a table covered with a red or blue cloth, and the yellow seems to intensify; place it where the flowers are viewed against mauve, and they positively glow.

Take, as another example, a bunch of bright red flowers, scarlet dahlias, for instance, and you might think that, no matter what the furnishing scheme, they would pack the most powerful colour punch possible. They

would, if placed against green, but their brilliance would be visually diluted if moved in front of an orange wall or a mauve curtain. And so the message is clear: if you want to create a real, visual, impression with a gift of red roses, surround them with green foliage, or tie them with a big green ribbon bow.

The cause of this effect is most readily understood by reference to what is known as a colour wheel, representing the sequence of colours as they are seen in the rainbow, and as they relate to one another. The theory of the use of colour can help you to choose flowers in the single colour most likely to create a vibrant or restrained effect in any part of the home, and to select floral blends that harmonize or perfectly complement each other.

The wheel is divided into six segments. Each of the alternate sections is made up of the three primary colours: red, blue, and yellow. Between those are the secondary colours, the ones which result from mixing the primaries: mauve by blending red and blue, green derived from blue and yellow, and orange resulting from a red and yellow

*Familiarity with the colour
wheel will help you to choose
flower colours to create a
particular effect. The large
wheel is divided into six
sections, showing the primaries
– red, yellow, and blue – and
the colours derived from
mixing them. The smaller
colour wheels illustrate the
complementary colours – those
opposite one another on the
wheel. Used together,
complementary colours are
seen to best advantage.*
Opposite

*Flowers for a garden room or
working conservatory can have
a high degree of informality.
Arranged in a pottery watering-
can, the orange marigolds and
nasturtiums contrast with the
blue love-in-a-mist and pansies
to create a complementary
scheme.* **Below**

blue jug with a towering partnership of bright orange Chinese lanterns (winter cherry), fresh or dried, midnight-blue larkspur, and misty-blue sea holly; combine blue iris in a springtime group with marmalade-orange narcissus and tulips; or, later in the year, mix blue Michaelmas daisies with rusty chrysanthemums and autumn leaves in a copper jug.

The interpretation of this complementary-colour pairing, the 'Complete Harmony' arrangement, was inspired by a modern oil painting, and grew from there. Not everyone happens to have containers in just the right colours for a scheme: for this arrangement two stone mustard jars were drizzle-painted and filled with lilies, larkspur, iris and anemones, with a cluster of pyracantha (firethorn) berries for extra glow and contrasting texture.

The equally vibrant mauve-and-yellow partnership could be interpreted in a variety of moods; with the pretty springtime pairing of pale primroses and deep purple

mix. To take the illustration a stage further, each segment may be divided into sections to represent the strength of the colour, from the deepest shades when the colour is mixed with black, to the palest pastel tints when it is blended with white in varying degrees. With this colour tool, you can evaluate the effect each colour has on its neighbour, and the effect each flower or group of flowers would have on its companions in an arrangement.

To put the theory to the test, there is no need to gather a basketful of flowers in all colours of the rainbow, or to make a lavish experimental purchase at the florists . Cut out coloured blocks from a magazine or use small paint samples, shuffling them into various pairings and groups – deepest violet with palest blue, a pleasant harmony; pale pink with bright orange, warm but not particularly strident; bright blue with brilliant orange, an exercise in going for bold.

COMPLEMENTARY HUES

When two colours that oppose each other on the wheel are used together, in full strength, the outlook is dazzling: primary blue and secondary orange; primary yellow and secondary mauve; primary red and secondary green. These pairings, which illustrate the attraction of colour opposites and speak volumes in impact terms, are known as complementary, or contrasting.

To take the blue-and-orange combination as an exercise in scene-stealing arrangements, you could fill a tall,

YULETIDE DISPLAYS

Sometimes it may be a favourite container, sometimes a particular background, sometimes the seasonal availability of the plant materials, or sometimes tradition that suggests arrangements in certain colour pairings. Can it be coincidence or is it simply luck that at Christmastime both tradition and the range of plant materials available to us – all the glowing tints and shades of evergreens and the contrasting brightness of their berries – lead us to deck our homes in the complementary-colour pairing of red and green?

In celebration of the festival, you may choose to arrange a few sprays of variegated leaves and scarlet berries in a still-life group with a trio of red candles; combine the softness of a grey-green plant such as ballota with glossy green ivy and holly; or gather together the brightest flowers of the season, be they poinsettia, carnations, or anemones, in a jade-green jug or a bright red biscuit or cookie tin. Whatever your choice, you can be sure that you have both tradition and colour balance on your side.

A green and white arrangement looks suitably seasonal at Christmas, an echo of frost and snow covering the evergreens outside. The table design, which combines white freesias, roses, and spray carnations with holly and snowberries, is tied with green ribbons. **Left**

A natural container for a farmhouse setting – the loaf is hollowed out and the shell baked until it is dry. It is then fitted with a liner and soaked foam and filled with a flourish of flowers in sunshine colours – carnations, marigolds, Peruvian lilies, and marjoram. **Opposite**

A host of orange marigolds combined with soft, fluffy sprays of goldenrod creates a bright and casual composition in colours which are adjacent on the colour wheel. This simple grouping forms a perfect visual link between the home and the garden, and would strike a welcoming note on the breakfast table. **Right**

violets arranged in bunches in a wooden basket. You could gather the flowers into a posy, tie the stems with a handful of raffia, and place them in a mauve or yellow container or, for a touch more originality, in a scooped-out lemon fitted with a small water-holding container. This is similar to what has been done in the 'Perfect Complement' arrangement. The container, a hollowed-out melon shell, gave the lead for the colour-coordinated scheme, a luxuriant complement of orchids and carnations together with fluffy mimosa, high-sheen lilies, and soft-petalled roses.

Adjacent shades

At the other end of the impact scale are the colour pairings, descriptively termed adjacent, that are next to each other on the colour wheel and considered to be harmonious, even restrained. Red and mauve, mauve and blue, and so on around the wheel indicate the pairings or groupings that are closely related. This harmony is perfectly illustrated by a cluster of anemones, all the reds, mauves, and blues blending together, with each colour playing an equal part in the whole arrangement; or, in a sunnier vein, by a bunch of dahlias in brilliant orange, yellow, and red, arranged for the greatest impact in a black container.

Alternate shades

The third group of colour pairings, the alternates – those that are one place away from each other on the wheel – are considered more difficult to use with ease in floral designs; this applies especially to full-strength red and yellow, orange and mauve. But there are times when you may want an arrangement which positively commands attention in colour terms. The occasion may arise at the height of summer, when a floral display for a party in the garden has to compete with the deep blue of the sky and the brilliance of the sun; at the New Year, when everyone is in party mood and the flowers have to match it; or, indeed, at any large informal gathering, when an arrangement has to be seen across a crowded room. At such times a basket painted deep purple and filled with a mass of purple and lemon-yellow statice, or a red enamel container burgeoning with scarlet and yellow lilies could perfectly capture the mood of the moment.

STEP-BY-STEP FLOWER ARRANGEMENTS

~

You may have been asked to arrange the flowers for a church festival or a friend's wedding; you may want to give your home an extra sparkle for a party or at Christmas, or you may simply wish to brighten your home with a glorious profusion of flowers and foliage. Whatever the occasion, the projects on the following pages are certain to fill every requirement.

Concise, informative text, and step-by-step photographs will take you through every stage. Wiring and taping stems; fitting containers with wire mesh netting or stem-holding foam; fixing plant material to a ring base or making a garland – all the preparation and techniques required are clearly demonstrated, ensuring exquisite results every time.

ROMANTIC INTERLUDE

A beautiful old hand-painted jug, surely a family heirloom, was the keynote of this uncompromisingly romantic bedside group. The subtle scents of summer's prettiest blooms – roses, carnations, and freesias – mingle to become a fresh-flower potpourri.

1 Pale pink and partly-opened roses, which form a more attractive composition than tightly-furled buds, form the heart of the design and echo the pattern on the container. Glossy highlights are provided by the shiny petals of the sharp yellow lilies and the trumpet-shaped freesias. The short foliage sprays, which will be arranged in a ring around the rim of the jug, give the flower group a natural, straight-from-the-garden look.

2 Crumple the wire mesh netting into a ball and fit it into the neck of the jug, so that it forms a mound extending above the rim. Criss-cross two pieces of adhesive tape, threading them through the netting and sticking the ends to the container. Check the netting is held firmly in place. Position a tall stem of foliage at the back of the container, and a ring of roses through the centre.

3 Continue the group by positioning more roses, their stems cut to varying lengths so that the flowers are graduated in height. Begin positioning the lilies between the roses, the large star-shaped flowers contrasting with the full, compact ones.

4 Add more lilies, at varying heights throughout the arrangement, then the carnations and the freesias, cutting some stems short so that the flowers rest close to the rim of the container.

5 Add the soft, feathery foliage throughout the design, so that it separates some of the flowers and allows them to be seen in clear outline. Arrange some short stems of foliage around the rim of the jug, where it will conceal the mound of wire mesh netting.

ORIENT EXPRESS

An elegant blue and white patterned vase suggests a composition in the traditional Oriental flower colours of yellow, white and blue. Simplicity is the key. The three flower types are complemented with delicate sprays of ming foliage.

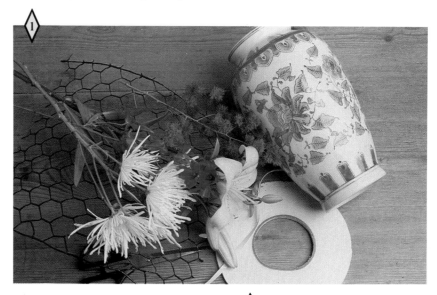

1 Choose flowers in clear, crisp colours and in shapes that contrast sharply with each other. Designs inspired by those of the Orient should have clear, uncluttered lines and the plant material should be well-defined.

2 Crumple the wire mesh netting into a ball and shape and press it into the neck of the container. Thread two strips of florists' adhesive tape through the wires and cross them over the mound and onto the container rim. Cut the stems of the lilies in varying lengths, so that the flower heads will range in height.

3 Position the stems of the spider chrysanthemums so that the flower clusters form a ring around the lilies, concealing some of their stems.

4 Add the blue accents, the delphinium flowers that echo the colour of the vase decoration. These flowers nestle against the lily stems, partially concealing them.

5 Arrange the stems of ming foliage around the rim of the vase. Position a few stems of pampas grass foliage at one side of the arrangement, to cascade over the vase.

THE WILD LOOK

You Will Need

tall, wide basket • waterproof liner such as a plastic bowl • block of absorbent stem-holding foam, soaked in water • narrow florists' adhesive tape • scissors • selection of materials such as drying oak leaves, dried arbutus leaves, dried poppy seedheads, teasels, wheat, old man's beard, rosehips, rose 'mossballs' • secateurs (pruning shears) • clear varnish (optional)

As winter approaches it is both exhilarating and rewarding to set off in search of countryside treasures. You may find oak leaves turning from green to yellow, vibrant rosehips and haws, a few stray stalks of wheat, dried poppy seedheads and teasels, and fluffy tufts of old man's beard (*Clematis vitalba*) – enough to compose a basket to set in the garden room or anywhere that will catch shafts of autumn sunlight.

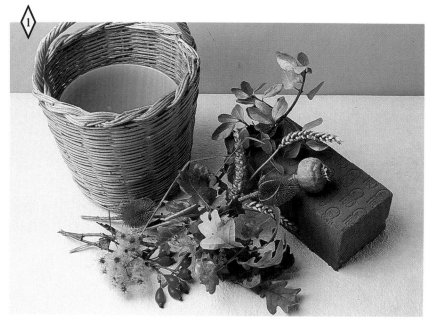

1 A craftsman's basket was chosen for this design – one traditionally used by Greek olive pickers. Its close, even weave and almost smooth texture lends itself to the overall effect. A more rustic and rugged container might overshadow the neutral tones and subtle textures of the wayside materials. Gather as many of the rosehips as you can, the brighter the better.

2 Place the plastic bowl or other liner in the basket and put the block of soaked foam in place. It can be secured in position by taking adhesive tape from side to side and front to back, over the foam and down on the basket

rim. Position the first stems of oak, the tallest one off-centre at the back and another, well curved and twisted, low over the front on the same side. Position a short stem of oak leaves at the front on the opposite side.

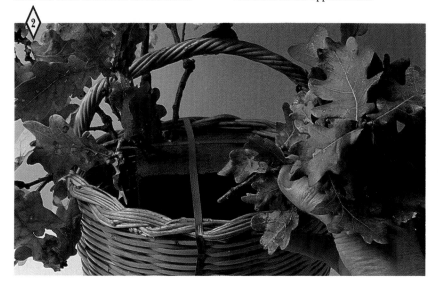

3 Add the tall stem of contrasting leaves, in this case dried and sun-bleached arbutus. Then arrange a cluster of wheat stalks. The ones chosen here curved naturally to one side, arching over the basket rim and giving the impression of a field of wheat swaying in the breeze.

4 The textural contrast builds up. Add teasels of varying lengths, the furry 'mossballs' from a wild rose bush, and the dried poppy seedheads. Cut some stems short so that the plant material rests against the basket rim.

5 Position the rosehips in clusters as dense as your supply will allow. The arrangement benefits from a generous profusion of the rich, glossy red colour. If you wish, paint or spray the berries with clear varnish.

6 Complete this wild-looking and asymmetrical design by adding short sprays of fluffy old man's beard where they will contrast strikingly with the solid shapes of the poppy seedheads and the high gloss of the rosehips.

7 The addition of three full-blown pink roses, the last ones of summer, provides contrast to a design composed principally of neutral tones.

SHEER ELEGANCE

You Will Need

tall, shapely jug ● *piece of plastic-covered wire mesh netting*
● *narrow florists' adhesive tape*
● *scissors* ● *selection of flowers such as* Euphorbia fulgens, *larkspur, and roses* ● *foliage such as eucalyptus* ● *florists' scissors*

A container with classic lines suggests a stylish but uncluttered composition that in no way detracts from the distinctive pattern. The use of a foam-holding saucer and a cylinder of soaked foam enables the stems to be angled in a curve that echoes the lines of the jug.

1 The flowers are chosen to emphasize and complement the colours of the Gothic-style pattern on the jug. The *Euphorbia fulgens* is a bright interpretation of the rust-red arches, the blue of the larkspur a lighter version of the background colour, and the roses a slightly richer shade of the cream of the figures.

3 Begin adding the blue flowers, to provide rich contrast with the euphorbia. Tall, stately stems of delphinium or larkspur occupy the centre ground of the design and form a dense background for the delicate cream roses.

2 Crumple the wire mesh netting into a ball and fit it into the neck of the container. Ease the wire upwards so that it forms a mound extending above the neck of the jug. Thread two strips of adhesive tape through the wire, criss-cross it over the mound and stick the ends onto the container. Arrange arching stems of the euphorbia, cut to varying lengths, so that the vibrant flowers and leaves cascade over one side of the jug.

4 Cut the rose stems to varying lengths and split or cut the stem ends so that the flowers will have the best chance of a long vase-life. Position the stems so that the flowers form a fan shape at the front of the arrangement.

5 Complete the arrangement by positioning some foliage stems to arch over the handle of the jug and balance the cascade of euphorbia. This will prevent a lop-sided look. Cut off any euphorbia leaves that look particularly wayward and may spoil the overall shape of the design.

THE MODERN APPROACH

A tall, wide cylindrical vase spatter-painted to harmonize with the wall behind it is on just the right lines for a low-key floral display in a modern setting. The flowers and foliage stems are arranged so that the materials form a dense, closely-integrated pattern, light materials against dark ones, stately lilies contrasting with delicate roses.

1 The most striking feature of this design is not the lilies, but the large, deep green and glossy acanthus leaves which allow all the flowers to be seen in sharp outline. You could substitute fig, *Fatsia japonica* or hosta (plantain lily) leaves, among others, to create a similar effect. In place of the pampas grass leaves you could use slender stems of broom.

3 Position the lily stems so that the fully-opened flowers are pointing in different directions – some forward, some to the right, and some to the left. In this way you can appreciate the full beauty of these flowers in silhouette.

2 Crumple the wire mesh netting into a ball and fit it into the neck of the container. Thread two lengths of adhesive tape through the netting, criss-cross them over the container and stick the ends close to the rim, where they will be concealed by the lowest of the plant materials. Arrange the acanthus stems so that the leaves form a bowl shape to outline the flowers, with the tallest stems at the back and the lowest ones at the front.

4 Cut off all but the top-most rose leaves, to prevent a crowded mass in the heart of the design. Split the ends of the rose stems to facilitate water intake.

5 Arrange the roses so that they nestle among the lily stems and give an overall roundness to the design. Add short sprays of foliage, such as eucalyptus, to trail over the container rim, and a few strands of pampas foliage at one side.

COUNTRY STYLE

You Will Need

large jug or vase • *piece of plastic-covered wire mesh netting*
• *narrow florists' adhesive tape*
• *scissors* • *selection of flowers such as marigolds, goldenrod delphinium, and* Euphorbia fulgens
• *florists' scissors* • *secateurs (pruning shears)*

A medley of cottage-garden flowers vividly contrasting in shape, texture, and colour are arranged just as they might grow in a border – intermingled and in profusion. The jug, a junk shop find, was crackle-painted to match the wall.

1 To achieve this country look, choose flowers which contrast with each other in every way. These can vary according to season.

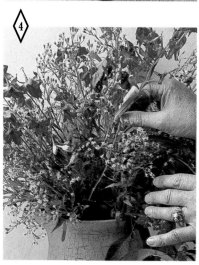

2 Crumple the wire mesh netting into a ball and fit it into the neck of the jug so that it forms a mound above the rim. Criss-cross two pieces of adhesive tape over the wire, threading them through it in several places and sticking the ends to the container. Arrange the arched stems of euphorbia so that they droop over the jug handle, on one side only.

3 Arrange the goldenrod stems so that they form a pyramid shape, with the tallest ones in the centre and progressively shorter ones at the front and sides.

4 Position the delphinium stems among the goldenrod and towards the back of the design. Some stems should be long enough for the contrasting blue flowers to be seen in detail against the yellow.

5 Arrange the round, flat-faced marigold flowers at varying heights so that they are seen in a circular formation. Select the best, brightest specimen to place in the centre front, where it will overlap the rim of the jug. In a more formal arrangement, this would be considered the focal point.

TRADITIONAL VALUES

A two-handled glass urn, the type of container popular in 18th-century compositions, holds a classic combination of flowers in pastel tints of pink, peach, and cream. The romantic roses contrast well with the trumpet shapes of the Peruvian lilies and freesias.

1 To achieve the near-symmetry of the arrangement, which is broken only by a couple of stems of freesia placed low over the rim, you need a balanced container, one with two handles, or no handles at all. An urn-shaped vase would be equally suitable. If possible, include some foliage which is variegated, so that it contributes to the lightness of the design.

2 Cut short lengths of adhesive clay and press onto the underside of the plastic saucer. Press the saucer onto the rim of the container. Position the cylinder of soaked foam in the saucer indent, and secure it in place by criss-crossing two strips of adhesive tape over the foam and the saucer and sticking the ends on the container. Arrange the various types of foliage to form the outline of the design, with some stems trailing low over the rim of the container on each side. Cut short sprays of the flowering shrub and arrange them between the sprays of variegated foliage, emphasizing the triangular shape of the outline.

3 Arrange long stems of a slender foliage type to give height to the design. If you wish the arrangement to conform to formal lines, the foliage tips should be confined to the triangular shape. Longer, more wayward-looking stems add a touch of informality.

4 Cut individual stems from some of the Peruvian lilies and position them at the heart of the design, close to the foam and among the sprays of flowering shrub. Arrange longer stems within the triangular outline.

5 Fill in the design with partly-opened roses, reserving the prize bloom for the centre front position, low over the container rim.

6 Arrange the freesias between the roses where their differing shapes and tints will form a flattering contrast. Arrange short stems of foliage such as eucalyptus at the heart of the design and, for a finishing touch, add a couple of stems of foliage and freesias slanting almost vertically to one side.

A BOLD STATEMENT

The boldest statement you can make is to arrange flowers in the three primary colours – red, yellow, and blue – at full strength. This eye-catching arrangement is suitable for an entrance hall or a landing, or as the centre-piece of a buffet table where the party is in full swing.

1 If possible, choose a plain container in one of the flower colours, or one with a bold pattern in primary colours. A yellow enamel salad bowl was used here, to match the brilliance of the mimosa.

2 Crumple the wire mesh netting and fit it into the bowl. Cut short strips of adhesive tape, wrap one end around the wire close to the rim, and bring the tape over and along the vessel, just inside the rim. Repeat this around the bowl to secure the wire and check that it has no freedom of movement. Lightly crush the ends of the mimosa stems, scrape off about 5cm (2in) of the bark and split the ends with a sharp knife. Arrange the mimosa evenly around the container to create a dome shape.

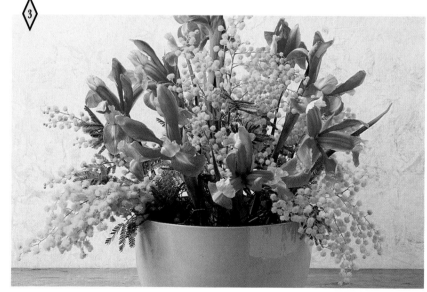

3 Cut the iris stems to different lengths and arrange them so that the colour is evenly distributed throughout the design, and the height is graduated.

4 The design features five red
carnations. Arrange them to
create a pyramid effect with the colour
evenly balanced throughout the group.

5 Arrange a few red anemones close
to the rim of the container where,
against the yellow of the bowl, they will
provide the sharpest contrast of all.

COMPLETE HARMONY

You Will Need

thick, sturdy container such as a mustard jar or other earthenware pot • florists' adhesive clay • scissors • plastic foam-holding saucer • cylinder and small piece of absorbent stem-holding foam, soaked in water • narrow florists' adhesive tape • selection of plant materials such as lilies, irises, anemones, larkspur, flowering shrub, pyracantha (firethorn) berries, spiky evergreen leaves • florists' scissors • secateurs (pruning shears)

In this design, primary blue and secondary orange, colours which face each other on the colour wheel, demonstrate the attraction of opposites. The composition was inspired by the modern abstract painting in the background; it would look equally dramatic against a plain blue or orange wall and positively brilliant against green.

1 The arrangement is designed as an exuberant burst of colour, like rays of the sun radiating from the central point. The lilies and irises, which both form star-like shapes, contribute to this effect. The two mustard jars, one used as the container and the other as an accessory, have been painted with enamel, the paint drizzled and left to run in uneven lines.

2 Cut short lengths of the adhesive clay and press onto the underside of the plastic saucer. Press the saucer onto the top of the container. Put the soaked foam cylinder in place in the saucer indent and secure it with two criss-crossing strips of adhesive tape taken over the foam and saucer and stuck onto the top of the container. Arrange the foliage stems to make a fanburst shape, the tallest ones at the back and shorter ones on either side. Position the stems of pyracantha (firethorn) berries low on one side of the design. Cut short lengths of the flowering shrub and place close against the foam. Position the first of the blue flowers in a fan shape.

3 The dramatic colour is already apparent. Place the iris stems well apart so that the flowers will not appear crowded in the finished arrangement. Position the anemones, the only round, flat flower shapes, low at the front of the design.

4 Cut off some of the lily leaves, to avoid a confusion of foliage. Cut the stems in varying lengths so the flowers will be equally balanced throughout the arrangement. Add more foliage stems to create a visual dividing line between the flowers.

5 Cut two short stems of iris and push them into the small piece of soaked stem-holding foam. When the arrangement is in position in the room, place the second container beside it, and conceal the foam in its depths, so that the flowers appear to be spilling out of the jar.

RED ALERT

You Will Need

tall, straight-sided container, such as a biscuit (cookie) tin or wine carafe • florists' adhesive clay • plastic foam-holding saucer • cylinder of absorbent stem-holding foam, soaked in water • narrow florists' adhesive tape • scissors • selection of flowers such as Euphorbia fulgens, carnations, spray carnations, and flowering shrub • stems of eucalyptus • florists' scissors • secateurs (pruning shears)

High drama is achieved by arranging flowers in a single hue, especially when the container – in this case a stylish biscuit (cookie) tin – strikes the same note. The addition of the white flowering shrub brings a touch of freshness to the design, and allows the full, rounded shape of the carnations to be seen in clear outline.

1 If possible, choose stems of the euphorbia, or a substitute flower, which have graceful curves, some to one side and some the other. The cascade effect this creates is important to the finished design. Three carnations are all you need to achieve a good visual balance, with sprays of their smaller counterparts, in a similar colour, serving as fillers.

2 Cut short strips of the adhesive clay and press onto the underside of the plastic saucer, where it will come into contact with the neck of the container. Press the saucer onto the top of the container and press the cylinder of soaked foam into the saucer indent. Secure the stem-holding material by criss-crossing two lengths of adhesive tape over the foam and the saucer and sticking them onto the top of the container. Cut the stems of eucalyptus to graduated lengths and position so that they arch in a small cascade on either side of the container. Arrange sprays of the flowering shrub to form a triangular outline above the container.

3 Cut the euphorbia stems in pairs of equal lengths and arrange on each side of the container to form a floral cascade, following the lines set by the eucalyptus. Cut off any wayward leaves that detract from the shape.

4 Arrange three carnations in a triangle, one at the top of the design, one slightly shorter on one side and one even shorter on the other. Begin filling in the gaps with stems of spray carnation.

5 Complete the arrangement by adding more spray carnations and stems of slender and pointed foliage. Be sure to place some stems so that the leaves trail down almost vertically, partially obscuring the tin. When a container has such a distinctive pattern as this one, with bold lettering, the flowers, even red ones, are in danger of being overshadowed by comparison.

6 When similar flowers are arranged in a jade green jug, the design becomes 'complementary' – a blend of two opposing colours on the colour wheel, each of which shows the other to best advantage. A composition like this, vibrant in its harmonious use of red and green, is particularly effective at Christmastime.

BLUE AND MAUVE

This casual yet radiant arrangement spans the divisions between blue and mauve, two neighbouring colours on the colour wheel. The patterned coffee pot, in rich creamy yellow, is integrated into the design by the yellow flashes of the irises.

1 Grey-green foliage such as eucalyptus blends especially well with the mauve and blue floral scheme. Other good choices would be ballota and senecio, with purple sage used as a filling material.

2 Cut two strips of adhesive clay and press onto the base of the saucer. Press the saucer onto the top of the container. Position the foam in the saucer and secure it with two lengths of adhesive tape, taken over the foam and onto the container. The eucalyptus stems are arranged in a lop-sided triangular shape to create the design outline. Short sprays of flowering shrub are placed close to the foam .

3 Arrange the irises among the foliage, to follow the outline and reinforce the shape of the design.

4 Arrange the anemones between the irises, so that the deep purple and blue flowers alternate to create the colour harmony. Among the bunch of anemones is a two-tone flower, placed centrally, as the focal point.

5 Position the freesias to form a cascade effect on one side, the flowers dipping low over the handle of the pot and following the line of the foliage. Fill in any gaps with short sprays of foliage.

6 The same arrangement with daffodils in place of the anemones. When deep violet is replaced by brilliant yellow, the colour-wheel opposite of mauve, the design becomes 'complementary' or 'contrasting', taking on a new and vivid brightness. Sprays of mimosa reinforce the springtime brilliance.

A PERFECT COMPLEMENT

When mauve and yellow, two opposite colours on the colour wheel, are arranged together the result is sure to be both high-profile and eye-catching. Add to the impact of the design by using a scooped-out melon, with its deeply-ridged texture, as the unusual container.

1 Fruits and vegetables make interesting short-term containers; you can dry the shells in an oven at low temperature for a more permanent display. Watermelons, pumpkins and marrows (squash), or oranges and lemons can also be used.

Choose flowers which contrast dramatically with each other in both shape and texture – the huge, glossy yellow lilies and the tiny fluffy mimosa flowers are perfect examples.

2 Cut a thin slice from the top of the melon, and a sliver from the base so that it will stand steadily. With the spoon, scoop out the melon seeds into a bowl. Scoop out the melon flesh into a second bowl, taking care not to pierce and damage the shell.

3 Press the plastic saucer over the top of the melon and press the soaked foam into the indent. Criss-cross two lengths of adhesive tape over the foam and saucer and down onto the melon shell. Arrange stems of mimosa to make an irregular shape.

4 Arrange the orchids to make a triangular outline, the tallest one in the centre and two slightly shorter stems at the sides. Position the carnations to give weight to the design at the top and sides. Cut the lily stems and position them at the heart of the design, where the fully-opened flowers will be seen head on.

5 Add the cream roses, positioning some at the back so that they will be viewed through the more prominent flowers, and one low at the right. Complete the design with light sprays of foliage, placing some on the left of the arrangement to balance the rose. Keep the foam permanently moist, adding water at least once a day.

HOGARTH CURVE

You Will Need

*tall, slender container such as a
candlestick or figurine vase*
● *florists' adhesive clay* ● *scissors*
● *small waterproof container for
foam (a plastic foam-holding saucer
may be too large for many designs)*
● *block of stem-holding foam, cut
to shape and then soaked* ● *knife*
● *narrow florists' adhesive tape*
● *curved foliage stems such as
broom to create the outline*
● *other foliage such as smilax,
variegated scented geranium, and
flowering shrub* ● *flowers such as
carnations, spray carnations, and
spray chrysanthemums* ● *florists'
scissors*

The design is named after the 18th-century English painter William
Hogarth, who called the flowing curves 'the line of beauty'. The stems
creating the upper and lower curves should be placed so the outline
appears as one rhythmic and unbroken line, sometimes known as a
'lazy S'. The design may be composed so that the curve flows from
either the right or the left.

1 It is important to select or coax
foliage or flower stems into
matching curves to form the outline of
the design. These broom stems were
twisted into a circle, secured with
rubber bands, and left overnight. More
substantial stems may need to be soaked
first, to make them supple.

2 Cut two short lengths of adhesive
clay, press onto the underside of
the foam holder and press the holder on
top of the container. Position the foam
in the container. Tape from side to side
and front to back, over the foam and
onto the candlestick. The outline of
the design begins to take shape, with
the clusters of broom stems placed
exactly opposite each other on either
side of the protruding cylinder of foam.
The delicate scented geranium leaves
reinforce the centre of the S-shape,
leaving the tips slender and wispy.

3 Cut the carnation stems short and
place one on either side and one
low at the centre front of the design,
where it will mask the container and
holding material.

4 Position two more carnations, one to create a central dome effect and the other at the back of the design. Cut short stems of spray carnations and position them to fill in the gaps and provide a colour contrast. Add spray carnations to follow the outline of the foliage.

5 Position short sprays of a light foliage, such as smilax, between the principal flowers, with others trailing low at the front and back of the design to mask every trace of the mechanics.

GEOMETRY LESSON

Whoever would have thought, when learning about right-angled triangles, that the knowledge would be put to use in a flower arrangement! This design, an interpretation of the classic L-shape, is composed on a stoneware dish which has, by contrast, gentle curves.

1 Select flowers that are well suited to a watery theme. Those with glossy or wax-like petals such as irises, lilies, and tulips seem to have a special affinity with designs in which 'open water' is a feature. Select sword-shaped foliage for the exaggerated point of the design; lily, tulip, and montbretia are among the many possibilities.

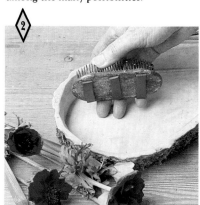

2 Make sure the inside of the container is absolutely dry. Cut three short lengths of florists' adhesive clay and press onto the bottom of the pinholder. Position this to one side of the container and press firmly in place.

3 Define the shape of the L with long, straight stems of foliage placed at right angles to one another. Note that the principal upright stem is a little way in from the edge of the pinholder. Give balance to the design by placing a shorter stem to the left of the principal stem with another angled to the right.

4 Position the irises, pressing the stems firmly onto the pinholder spikes, so that the flowers follow the shape outlined by the leaves.

5 Position the daffodils to fill in the gaps and complement the contrasting shape of the irises. Place a cluster of short-stemmed anemones close to the pinholder, where the flowers will be seen as deep shadows, and add a few foliage sprays. Spoon the concealing material – in this case broken windscreen (windshield) glass – around the pinholder until it is completely hidden. Glass has the advantage – over pebbles and granite, for example – of catching and reflecting the light in an attractive way.

6 This is a design which would be equally appropriate in both formal and informal surroundings. Here it is featured in a country setting, with a complementary bunch of raffia-tied irises displayed as a short-term and eye-catching accessory. You could also use a bunch of evergreens or dried flowers as a wall decoration.

GENTLE SLOPE

Composed on a spatter-painted wine carafe, the design forms a diagonal line, softened by the cluster of delicate and pretty flowers at the centre. A pair of such designs, raised on their pedestal-like containers above the table surface and composed as mirror images of each other, would be suitable decorations for a buffet or party table.

1 It is useful to have tall, narrow containers to compose angled and curved designs, and to decorate a party table when space is a consideration. This one, a discarded wine carafe, was painted white, left to dry and then splashed with coral pink, a colour which tones perfectly with the roses and carnations.

2 Cut strips of the adhesive clay and press onto the underside of the plastic saucer, where it will come into contact with the top of the container. Press the saucer in position, and place the soaked foam in the indent, securing it with two strips of adhesive tape criss-crossed over the foam and the saucer and stuck onto the container top. Define the line of the diagonal with two straight stems of foliage. Follow the outline with slender stems of spray carnations and strengthen it with the more rounded shapes of the roses.

3 Cut short sprays of goldenrod and place them slanting upwards on one side, and downwards on the other, to create a softened diagonal line. Cut one carnation stem very short and position it with the flower close against the foam.

4 Fill in the centre of the design with more carnations. Place short sprays of goldenrod to trail down over the rim of the container with others of a similar length making a gentle curve over the top. The effect is of an elongated oval.

5 Add short sprays of light foliage. To complete the design, cover the reverse. If it is to be viewed from all sides, arrange with a similar placement of flowers and leaves. If not, cover the foam and the plastic saucer with goldenrod, foliage, and just a few spray carnations.

ALL-ROUND SUCCESS

A design which is destined to be seen from all angles, as it would be in the centre of a dining table or occasional table, must be an all-round attraction. Turn the arrangement round one quarter of a circle as you compose it, and give it a final check to make sure it is worthy of every admiring glance.

1 We wanted a lush and luxurious look for this semi-formal centre-piece and chose a colour scheme in the rich, warm colours of velvet. A wide, bulbous pot was painted to give a feeling of 19th-century opulence. A brass, copper, or pewter pot, or any container in black, dark red, deep blue, purple, or forest green would be equally suitable.

2 Crumple the wire mesh netting into a ball and press it into the top of the container. Secure in place by threading two strips of florists' adhesive tape through the wire, criss-crossing them in the centre and sticking them to the top of the pot, where the ends will be concealed by the overhanging plant materials. Arrange the foliage to make a full shape all around the pot. Turn the container to check that the leaves are distributed evenly on all sides.

3 Work on one quarter of the arrangement at a time. Place short stems of euphorbia to arch over the side of the container at different levels. Position the anemones around the centre, alternating their colours to heighten the interest, and the spray carnations close to the container rim. Position the fully-opened roses at the heart of the design.

4 Compose the opposite side in a similar way, and fill in the gaps with short sprays of variegated foliage to separate the rich, deep colours of the flowers.

5 Turn the container around and repeat the design on the reverse, matching the first side in essence if not in detail. Polished wood makes a perfect surface for this rich-looking and jewel-bright arrangement.

INFORMAL TRIANGLE

A rectangular basket makes a perfect container for an informal arrangement on geometric lines – a triangular design in a country-style setting.

1 The arrangement is based on a classic triangular shape, with slender foliage stems and light weight sprays of goldenrod defining the points at the top and sides. For a more formal appearance, the basket could be replaced with a pottery or earthenware baking dish or a baking tin painted to suit the furnishings.

2 Place the liner in the basket, then the soaked foam. Hold the foam in place with two strips of florists' adhesive tape taken from front to back and side to side, stuck onto the container rim where it will be concealed by the plant materials. Position stems of foliage and sprays of goldenrod to define the outline of the design. To conform to the principles of a classic arrangement the height of the central stem should be at least 1½ times the longest measurement of the basket – in this case it is 35cm (13½in).

3 The cone-like shapes of the Peruvian lilies can be used to trace the pointed outlines of the design since they lead the eye naturally to the extremities. Cut the stems so that the flowers are positioned within those outlines, and cut off any leaves that would detract from the overall shape with their wayward curves. As always, cut the stems at a slanting angle, using sharp florists' scissors.

4 Position the carnations within the geometric outline, with two of the flowers placed close to the centre front of the design. Others should be positioned at the back of the arrangement, where they will be seen when the design is viewed from the sides. Fill in the gaps with spray chrysanthemums, with some individual flowers cut on short stems and placed close to the foam.

5 Complete the arrangement by filling in the gaps with goldenrod, the mass of tiny florets a softening influence on the more clearly defined outlines of the Peruvian lilies and roses.

STRAIGHT AND NARROW

You Will Need

rectangular container such as a plastic dish or metal baking tin • absorbent stem-holding foam, soaked in water • selection of flowers such as Singapore orchids, roses, carnations, and spider chrysanthemums • foliage such as montbretia • florists' scissors

An upright design verging on a classic vertical shape is ideal to display in a narrow alcove or niche; a pair of matching arrangements could enhance a sideboard or bookcase.

1 The quality and finish of the container you use is immaterial, since it is not seen in the finished design. Here a book will be used as a base, taking the place of a container to form a composite part of the arrangement. An old wooden or lacquered box could be used as a decorative stand in place of the book.

2 Place the soaked foam in the container. Outline the shape with the tallest, sword-shaped leaves of montbretia. It might be necessary to cut the ends to a point to make it easier to insert them into the foam. Arrange shorter stems of slender foliage to make a fan shape.

4 Cut short the carnation stems and position two of the flowers in a straight line, one above the other at the centre front, and one to one side.

5 Arrange cream orchids behind the purple ones, where they will give the design dimension and depth. Cut individual flowers from the stems of spider chrysanthemums and arrange them with the roses in a cluster around the base. Add a few stems of spray carnations at the middle height, and fill in any gaps with short sprays of foliage.

3 The deep purple orchids give the design a look of elegant luxury. Arrange them to follow the fan shape outlined by the green foliage. Position the stems so that the flowers are not touching each other; they should not look cramped or crowded.

FIRST AMONG UNEQUALS

You Will Need

footed stand such as a cake plate
● *florists' adhesive clay* ● *scissors*
● *plastic foam-holding saucer*
● *cylinder of soaked foam*
● *narrow florists' adhesive tape*
● *foliage such as eucalyptus and
flowering shrub* ● *flowers such
as freesias, anemones, and
carnations* ● *secateurs (pruning
shears)*

An asymmetrical, or 'lop-sided' triangle is one of the classic geometric floral shapes. This arrangement, with deep coral pink two-tone carnations as the focal point, is well suited for display on a sideboard or side table.

1 A container with a slightly raised 'foot', facilitates an arrangement with side stems flowing downwards. You could equally well compose this design on a taller cake stand, or on a rectangular basket or wooden box in which the stem-holding foam extended about 5cm (2in) above the rim.

2 Cut two strips of adhesive clay and press onto the underside of the saucer. Press the saucer onto the stand, a little to the left of centre for a design that will flow to the right. Arrange the eucalyptus stems to etch in the height, with one tall, straight stem leaning slightly backwards and another, upright, in front of it. Position short stems flowing forwards on the left of the design with longer ones on the opposite side. Arrange the shorter stems of eucalyptus close to the centre, and others at the back of the design, to give balance and to cover the mechanics.

3 The freesias, with their narrow trumpet shapes, are used as 'points' in the design, following the outline of the triangle, with one in the centre to carry the colour through from the top to the bottom. The anemones, which are seen as small 'rounds', alternate with the freesias within the arrangement.

4 Position the three large 'rounds' – the carnations – to form the focal point, with one placed low and close to the rim of the container. Add more filler material – the flowering shrub – at the back of the design, where it will be seen through the foliage.

5 Complete the design with more short stems of flowering shrub and with forward-flowing stems of eucalyptus to break up the line of the container rim.

NAUTICAL THEME

You Will Need

*wooden box with a lid ● florists'
adhesive clay ● scissors ● small
waterproof container such as an
upturned coffee jar lid ● slice
cut from a cylinder of absorbent
stem-holding foam, soaked in water
● wooden cocktail sticks (if
needed) ● selection of flowers such
as irises, spray chrysanthemums,
and spray carnations ● foliage such
as eucalyptus ● florists' scissors*

A brass-lidded box opens to reveal a horizontal display with a nautical flavour. This design, with flowers in blue, bronze, and white, is suitable for a man's desk, and is narrow enough to be placed on a bookshelf.

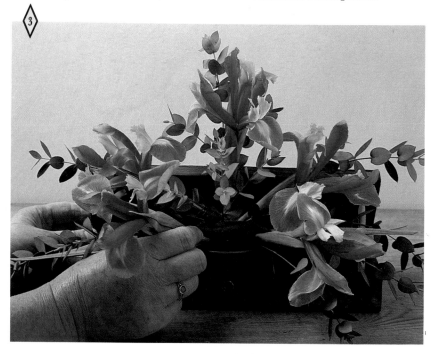

1 The brass-lidded box gives character to the arrangement, though the glint of the metal cannot be seen from a straight-on view. You could use a sewing or needlework box, a child's pencil box, or a paintbox for a similar effect. You need a small waterproof holder for the foam slice – a purpose-made plastic saucer is too large for such a narrow arrangement.

2 Cut strips of adhesive clay and press to the underside of the foam holder, where it will come into contact with the divisions in the box. Press the foam holder firmly in place. Wedge the box open with the cocktail sticks if needed. Position stems of eucalyptus to make a long, low, trailing shape. The tallest central stem should define the outline of a low triangle.

3 Position the irises within the outline defined by the foliage. Some of the flowers should slant downwards and forwards on either side of the stem-holding foam.

4 Arrange the spray carnations around the irises, positioning the pencil-thin buds at the points of the design.

5 Fill in the gaps with the round, flat flowers. In this example, bronze spray chrysanthemums were used, their colour echoing the flash on the iris petals.

RAISED ALOFT

You might have been asked to arrange a pedestal in church for Easter or a spring wedding, or at a public hall for a formal reception. Or you might like to compose a floral design on a stand to decorate the hall or a corner of a room for a special party. This design combines some of the loveliest blossoms and flowers of the season, in the traditional colours of the Easter festival.

1 The wrought-iron pedestal stand used for this design, with an adjustable stem, is already fitted with a dish-shaped metal container to hold stem-holding foam. If you use one which has a flat top, and requires an additional waterproof container, you can prepare it using the method described earlier.

3 Position sprays of lilac to follow the outline of the eucalyptus, one tall straight stem to reinforce the central height and others flowing outwards and downwards at the centre and sides. Position sprays of mimosa within the triangular shape.

2 Cut two short lengths of adhesive clay and press onto the underside of the two plastic prongs. Press these onto the base of the container, one to the back and one to the front of the centre point. Press two blocks of foam onto the prongs. Tape or wire over the foam and onto the container, parcel fashion, for extra security. Begin the outline of the triangular shape by positioning long stems of eucalyptus at the centre back and sides. Arrange stems of flowering shrub throughout the design, to form a natural-looking background for the flowers.

4 Arrange stems of lily in bud to
follow the points of the design,
and fully-opened flowers at the centre,
to create visual weight and interest.

5 Fill in the design with narcissus
arranged in clusters. Add short
sprays of mimosa as fillers, and a few
short sprays of pussy willow and catkins
to link the design with the countryside
in spring.

DAFFODIL WOOD

This Easter arrangement evokes one of the loveliest harbingers of spring – the sight of golden daffodils making a bright floral carpet under the bare branches of an apple tree. A piece of twisted and gnarled vinewood represents the tree, and the flowers and the twigs are positioned vertically, as if growing naturally. The arrangement could be positioned in a church porch, on the floor, or on a low wooden chest.

1 If you are not fortunate enough to find a shapely piece of wood in the countryside, it may be available from some florists' shops. As an alternative, to give the impression of a barren tree, you could use a handful of gnarled twigs – apple would be ideal – placed close together, the forked twigs facing in all directions.

2 Place the plate or other solid waterproof liner in the tray. Cut two strips of adhesive clay and press them onto the underside of the plastic prongs. Press them in position well apart on the liner, where they will anchor the main blocks of foam. Press two large pieces of foam onto the spikes and cut other pieces to fill in the circle around the edges. Cut a hole in the foam, towards the back and at one side, and push the vinewood into it. Twist two or three stub wires around the wood, twist the ends and press them at different angles into the foam, so that the 'tree' is held firmly in place.

3 Cover the foam with a thin layer of moss. Scrape away just enough of the moss to expose small areas, and press the daffodil stems vertically into the foam. Cut them to slightly varying heights to give the most natural effect.

4 Cut shorter stems of narcissus and arrange them in a group in front of the daffodils. Position stems of ivy to twine around the vinewood and trail through a clump of daffodils.

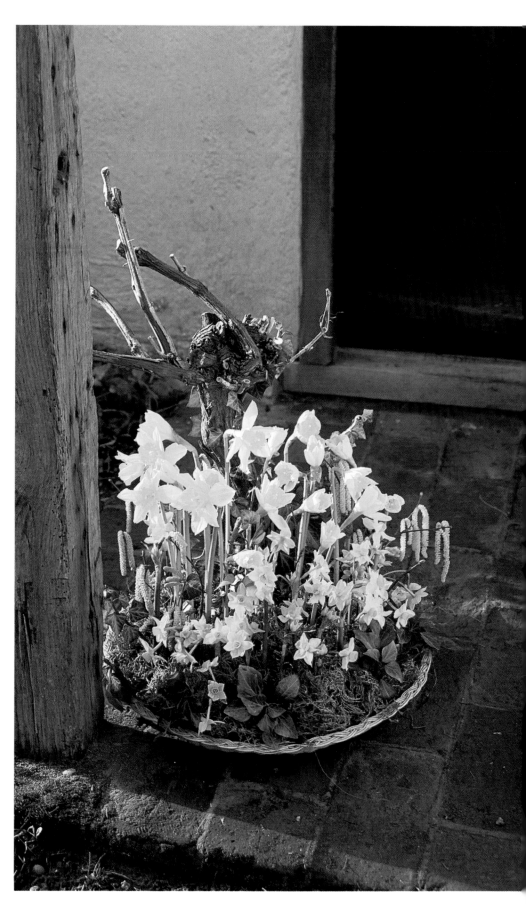

5 Position short sprays of ivy around the rim to edge and enclose the design and arrange a few stems with catkins to provide shape and texture variation.

MAY DAY WREATH

It's an old Greek custom to hang a colourful floral wreath, a *stefani*, on the door in celebration of the May Day festival. The decorations are composed of rings made of grass or other supple stems bound with a medley of wild and garden flowers. It is an idea well worth adopting for any occasion – just think what a warm welcome a flower ring would signal to party guests.

1 In the Greek tradition, the ring is composed of flower posies selected and arranged at random, not carefully matched and arranged symmetrically. Try to include some wild flowers if available. If the stems you cut to make the ring are too rigid to shape into a circle, soak them in water, then hang them in a bunch to dry.

2 Cut the stems to the length you require. This ring is 30cm (12in) diameter, made of stems 100cm (40in) long. Gather them into a neat bundle and pull out any which are particularly wayward. Wrap the twine around the stems, tie it into a knot and bind it over and around them. Overlap the ends to form a circle and bind securely, tying the twine and cutting off the end.

3 Sort the flowers into groups, those which will be bound into posies and others which will be added individually. Mix and match the flowers for the posies to give the most colourful and informal effect. Cut short the stems of the posy flowers and foliage and bind them with roll wire.

4 Using green twine or silver wire, bind on at random the flower posies and the individual flowers, so that the heads of each posy or separate flower head cover the stems and binding of the one before. It is not necessary to conceal every scrap of the stem ring, since it is a natural and authentic component of the design.

5 Continue binding on flowers to complete the colourful circle. Display it on a door, gate, or an internal or external wall.

VALENTINE TOKEN

You Will Need

heart-shaped woven basket
* *florists' adhesive clay* • *scissors*
* *waterproof holder* • *section cut
from a cylinder of absorbent
stem-holding foam to fit the holder,
then soaked in water* • *red roses
and rosebuds, and pink roses*
* *selection of foliage such as
eucalyptus, ming, and geranium*
* *florists' scissors*

For generations red roses have symbolized true love and red rosebuds, a traditional Valentine gift, young and ardent love. This arrangement composed in a heart-shaped basket, is the perfect way to 'say it with flowers'. Use the design as a table decoration when you are dining *à deux*, or give it as a meaningful token. A child's Valentine offering might include a posy of carnations and anemones.

1 Buy the roses at least a day before they are to be arranged, strip off the lower leaves, split the stem ends, and stand them in cool water. Select a variety of foliage, long sprays such as eucalyptus to outline the design, lightweight ming – or asparagus or maidenhair fern – as a filler, and heart-shaped leaves such as geranium to conceal the stem-holding foam.

3 Cut the stems of the roses and rosebuds to different lengths, and cut or split the stem ends so that the flowers will be able to take up water more readily. Position more rosebuds within the outline of the foliage.

2 Stick a small piece of adhesive clay to the base of the waterproof container; a small plastic pot is ideal. Press the holder to the base of the basket, close to the top on one side. Press the piece of soaked foam into the container; the foam should extend at least 1.5cm (½in) above the rim of the basket. Position the eucalyptus stems to outline the design – an irregular triangle – and position the rosebuds to follow those lines.

4 The pink roses, almost fully open, give the design a soft and more feminine appeal. Position the flowers among the red rosebuds, where their shape and colour contrast will be most significant.

5 Fill in the arrangement with more foliage, and place geranium leaves to cover every trace of the foam. The child's posy, a simple bunch of red anemones and carnations, is prettily tied with a scrap of lace trimming.

MOTHER'S DAY BASKET

You Will Need

shallow basket with a handle
● *waterproof liner such as a plastic*
box ● *block of absorbent*
stem-holding foam, soaked in water
● *narrow florists' adhesive tape*
● *scissors* ● *long-lasting foliage*
such as eucalyptus, and flowering
shrub ● *flowers such as roses and*
Peruvian lilies ● *florists' scissors*
● *secateurs (pruning shears)* ●
paper ribbon ● *stub wire*

What could be a more delightful surprise for a mother on her special day than a basket of roses and lilies, arranged with style and sent with love? The basket, painted to tone with the flowers, becomes a permanent keepsake. It would be ideal to hold wools, sewing materials, or bath preparations.

1 As the basket is so much part of the gift, choose a decorative one with care. The basket illustrated, with woven, twisted cane, was painted in uneven stripes of pink gloss paint, to add a touch of sparkle to the arrangement. This colour is repeated in the floral-printed paper ribbon bow, a flamboyant finishing touch to the design.

3 Arrange the roses to make a gently rounded shape, alternating the colours, pink and cream, so that each complements the other.

2 Put the liner in the basket and place the block of foam in it. Cut two strips of adhesive tape and criss-cross them over the foam and down onto the sides of the basket, to hold the foam firmly in place. Arrange the tallest stems of foliage to make a fan shape at the back of the basket. Cut progressively shorter stems for the centre and front, positioning them so they droop and trail over the rim.

4 Add the Peruvian lilies, cutting some individual flowers on short stems and positioning them close against the foam. Fill in the gaps with short sprays of flowering shrub.

5 Unfurl the twisted paper ribbon by pulling it out gently from one end. You need about 1m (1 yard) to make a full, generous bow.

6 Cut the length of ribbon required and tie it into a bow. Ease the loop until neat, and trim the ribbon ends by cutting them at a slant. Thread the stub wire through the back of the loop, twist and insert the two ends into the foam at the front of the basket. Spray the flowers with a fine mist of cool water, and keep the foam moist before you deliver your surprise gift.

HALLOWEEN HIGHLIGHT

You Will Need

piece of twisted vinewood, driftwood, or other well-shaped branch ● well-shaped, forked apple or other twigs, preferably covered with lichen ● small quinces, or golden apples or pears ● clear quick-setting glue or hot glue ● stub wires ● wire cutters ● small waterproof dish ● slice cut from a cylinder of absorbent stem-holding foam, soaked in water ● flowers such as single spray chrysanthemums ● pyracantha (firethorn) berries ● foliage such as ivy and berberis (barberry) ● florists' scissors ● secateurs (pruning shears) ● 2 apples ● apple corer ● 2 candles

Heighten the party atmosphere and brighten the buffet table with a forest of ideas for Halloween. This creation – which can be extended to any length desired – comprises a piece of gnarled and twisted wood, a bunch of apple twigs, and a small harvest of quinces. Add a handful of golden flowers, berries, and leaves and a couple of golden candlesticks, and you are all set to turn the lights down low.

1 To create the effect appropriate to Halloween, select the wood, twigs, and leaves with care. The more gnarled, twisted, forked, and green-encrusted the branches the better; the more purple and veined the ivy leaves, the more spooky the effect will be.

2 Begin by attaching the fruit to the twigs. You can do this in one of two ways, by gluing or wiring. If you decide to use glue, attach the fruits where the twigs fork and there is the largest area of contact. Cover the twig with glue or hot glue, press on the fruit and hold it in place for a few seconds until the glue sets.

3 If you prefer to wire on the fruits, push a stub wire through the back of each one, bring the two wire ends together and twist them firmly. Wrap the wire around a twig and twist the fruit until it rests neatly on the surface.

4 When you have given all the twigs a bountiful fruit crop, position them behind the horizontal branch. Glue the twigs to the wood and secure them in place with stub wires, if necessary, as the weight of the fruit makes the twigs top-heavy. Place the slice of foam in the holder and arrange a 'forest' of twigs and foliage stems, some positioned vertically and others horizontally, on either side.

5 Cut short sprays of the chrysanthemums and some separate flowers and arrange them in the foam. Add sprays of the autumn leaves – berberis (barberry) in this design – and more ivy leaves. The largest ones may be used to conceal the foam. Snip off any flowers that look too crowded or confusing.

6 Position the flower group at one end of the 'fallen branch' where it continues the line of the wood. Use an apple corer to scoop out the centre of the apples and insert a candle in each one. Keep lighted candles away from children or pets.

HARVEST-TIME

You Will Need

small pedestal stand • florists' adhesive clay • scissors • plastic bowl to hold a block of foam • absorbent stem-holding foam, soaked in water • narrow florists' adhesive tape • selection of flowers such as spray chrysanthemums, pom-pom chrysanthemums, lilies, goldenrod, and roses • selection of autumn foliage such as oak, copper beech, and hornbeam • florists' scissors • secateurs (pruning shears)

It's the time of the year when the gardens, markets, and florists' shops are brimming over with flowers in all the glorious colours of autumn, a time to fill homes and churches with a wonderful profusion of flowers. This design is for a small pedestal decorated with golden yellow, orange, and russet-brown flowers and foliage.

1 If you do not have access to a pedestal, you can compose the arrangement to stand on a small wine table or other occasional table. You could use foliage preserved in glycerin solution instead of the more brittle autumn leaves.

3 Balance the outline – and the weight of the arrangement – by positioning some foliage branches and flowers at the back. Cut thick stems at an angle, slant-wise, so that they can be inserted more easily into the foam. Build up the design by placing spray chrysanthemums to follow the triangular shape.

2 Stick strips of adhesive clay to the underside of the plastic container, and press it firmly onto the pedestal. Position the soaked foam in the container – the one used here has an indent purpose-made to fit the rectangular shape. Secure the foam and container to the pedestal by taking two strips of adhesive tape from side to side and front to back, sticking the ends under the platform of the pedestal. Begin by positioning foliage branches and goldenrod to make the triangular outline of the design.

4 Arrange some of the stems so that the flowers thrust forwards and downwards and trail below the top of the pedestal. It is especially important for large arrangements such as this to have a three-dimensional effect.

5 Position the lilies in the centre front of the arrangement, where they will become the focal point. Arrange roses, an attractive shape contrast, around them. Some of these, too, should slope downwards.

6 Add short sprays of goldenrod and autumn leaves as fillers. Place the pedestal where it is not likely to be knocked over – a niche in a corner of a room is ideal. Remember to top up the container with water every day to keep the foam permanently moist.

THANKSGIVING FESTIVAL

A rustic basket filled with flowers, fruit, and foliage can take its place with pride at a harvest festival or at Thanksgiving, and looks equally good in the home, chapel, or church. Set in a window, shafts of golden autumn sunlight will flatter the russet colours of the plant materials, or use the composition to bring a warm glow to a shadowy corner.

1 The colour scheme of the arrangement makes the most of the tints and tones of the season, from the near-purple of the blackberry leaves and sedum to the pale pink of the climbing roses and hydrangeas; from the rosy blush of the pomegranates to the apricot hue of the spray chrysanthemums.

2 Place the waterproof liner in the basket. Place one whole block of foam in the dish and a half block in front of it. Secure each block in place by taping it from side to side with adhesive tape, over the foam and onto the container. Take another strip from front to back, over both of the foam blocks. Arrange some tall stems and branches at the back of the basket – fruiting crab apple looks magnificent – and short stems at the front on the other side.

3 Prepare the fruits that comprise the focal point of the arrangement. Pomegranates were used here but rosy apples, pears, or bunches of grapes could be used instead. Thread a stub wire through the fruit, close to the base. Twist the wire firmly and bend a hook in one end, to loop over the basket rim or into the foam.

4 Position the pomegranates or other fruit at the front of the arrangement, one dipping low over the basket rim, one resting on it, and the other close to the foam.

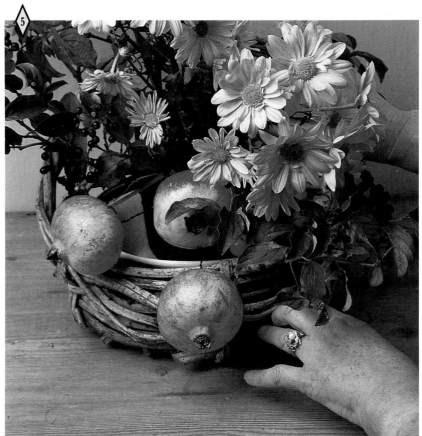

5 Cut the stems of the spray chrysanthemums to varying lengths and position them, tall, medium-height, and short, throughout the design.

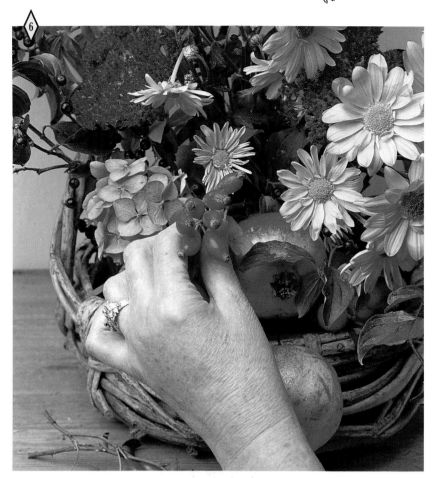

6 Begin to fill in the arrangement with the thick, ruby-red heads of sedum, which make a striking contrast to the neighbouring chrysanthemums. Add accents of glossy red rosehips, and pale pink hydrangeas.

7 Position partly-opened roses next to the rosehips, and blackberry stems to border the design on one side. Complete the design by adding short sprays of glossy ivy; the green leaves make an interesting contrast to the autumn tints.

8 In this bountiful season, this fruit and flower arrangement looks at its best surrounded by more autumnal crops. A generous pile of apples and pears, marrows and pumpkins, and the pick of the falling leaves all add to the look of plenty.

GARLAND OF EVERGREENS

The custom of bringing evergreens into our homes has its origins in the ancient world, when people believed them to have magical powers. A garland of evergreens, whether it is composed of blue pine, holly, or ivy, has the power to transform a corner of a room, a fireplace, or an arch and make it a decorative focal point at Christmastime.

1 This simple garland is composed of blue pine. Other materials could include Norwegian pine – the lower branches cut from the Christmas tree, perhaps – juniper, cypress, or many other evergreen species.

2 Measure the area where the garland is to hang, allowing for gentle curves and drapes and cut the rope to the required length. Tie the twine at one end of the rope. Take handfuls of hay or moss, wrap the material around the rope and bind it by taking the twine around it. Continue until the length, or lengths of rope are completely concealed beneath the natural material.

3 Cut the evergreen in short lengths and sprays. Place the first one over the hay-covered rope and bind it in place with the twine. Bind on more sprays, each one covering the stem end of the one before.

4 Gather the wheat in bunches of about six or seven heads and cut the stems to a total length of about 17.5cm (7in). Bind the stems with green twine. Place the bunches of wheat well apart on a newspaper and spray the heads with gold paint. Turn them over and spray them on the other side. Leave the paint to dry. Bind bunches of gilded wheat with the evergreens along the garland, first on one side and then the other.

5 When the length of the garland is completed, attach the cones. Drizzle spots of hot glue onto the pine at intervals and press on a cone. For the best appearance, alternate cones with long and rounded shapes.

6 Hang the garland in position and adjust it so that the evergreens, and not the hay-covered rope, are forward looking. Tie the ribbon into a bow, neaten the ends by cutting them at a slant, and thread the stub wire through the loop at the back. Attach the bow to the garland.

CHRISTMAS CHEER

Rose-coloured fruits and glossy nuts; gilded evergreens and glowing berries; coral carnations and vibrant roses – the materials bring together the natural gifts of the season in this outstanding Christmas decoration to display on a sideboard or side table, or as the centre of attraction on a buffet table.

You Will Need

large flat plate; the one used here is 30cm (12in) diameter • 2 plastic prongs • florists' adhesive clay • scissors • absorbent stem-holding foam, soaked in water • fruits, nuts, and berries such as pineapple, pomegranates, satsumas, lychees, pecans, and iris seeds • flowers such as carnations, roses, and spray chrysanthemums • evergreens such as ivy, yew, mahonia, eucalyptus, and cypress • florists' scissors • secateurs (pruning shears)

1 The deep coral shades of the pomegranate and the iris seeds provided the colour cue for this arrangement; the principal flowers – the carnations and roses – were chosen to fit in with the scheme.

2 Make sure the plate is absolutely dry. Cut two short strips of adhesive clay and press one onto the underside of each of the plastic prongs. Press these onto the plate, one just behind the central point and one in front of it and to the right. Push blocks of soaked foam onto the prongs. Begin the arrangement by positioning a selection of evergreens to outline the height on one side and the depth of the design on the other.

3 Put the pineapple in place at the front of the plate. As it leans against the larger block of foam it should not need fixing into place. Position the carnations and roses through the design with the taller stems at the back. Note that several of the flowers face outwards from the sides of the design.

4 Position stems of spray chrysanthemums behind the other flowers where they will be seen as fillers rather than feature flowers. Arrange the iris berries on tall, medium, and short stems to distribute their contrasting texture throughout the design. Arrange trails of ivy low at the front.

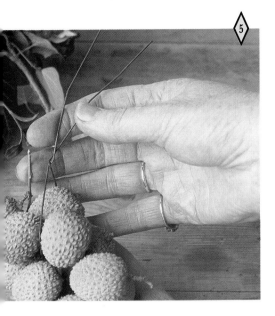

5 Using hot glue, or quick-setting clear glue, stick several lychees together in a deep cluster. Thread a stub wire through a gap between the fruits, position them close to the pineapple and push the wire into the foam. Glue a cluster of pecans and position in a similar way, on the opposite side. Thread a stub wire through the back of a satsuma, twist the two ends and push the wire into the foam above the cluster of lychees. Tuck a pomegranate under the cascade of fruits and another (not illustrated) behind the iris stems on the other side.

6 Complete the design by adding more sprays of evergreens including, perhaps, trails of ivy sprayed with gold paint. Cover all traces of foam at the back of the arrangement with sprays of cypress and ivy. Arrange piles of fruit close to the design to complete the effect.

KISSING RING

A bundle of wispy evergreens, clusters of gilded seedheads, a few sprigs of mistletoe, and two glittering bows make this the prettiest yuletide wreath ever. Hang it as a sign of welcome on the front door, on an internal wall or door or – a romantic notion – over a bed.

1 The wreath is designed to have an informal and slightly wayward look, so it is a good idea to avoid the darkest and heaviest of evergreens. Here, short sprays – hedge clippings – of lime-green cypress, slender trails of small-leafed ivy, eucalyptus, and mistletoe were used.

2 Cover the work surface with newspaper or scrap paper and spread out the wheat and linseed (flaxseed) seedheads, the artificial flowers, and any evergreens to be sprayed with gold paint. The degree of gilding in the design is a matter of personal preference. Here, a few of the ivy and eucalyptus stems were spatter-sprayed, but the leaves were not covered completely. Spray the materials on one side, then turn over and spray on the other. Leave to dry.

3 Gather the wheat into bunches of four or five stalks and bind them with silver wire. Gather the linseed (flaxseed) into bunches of uneven lengths – this gives the wispy look to the finished outline which is a feature of the design. Cut the evergreens into short lengths.

4 Cut several stub wires in half and bend them over to make U-shaped staples. Place a bunch of evergreens over the stem ring, loop a 'staple' over the stalks and press the wire ends into the wreath base.

5 Take a bunch of wheat and a piece of mistletoe, place so the heads cover the evergreen stems and staple in place. Continue adding evergreens and the other materials all around the ring, the heads of one cluster or bunch covering the stalks of the previous one.

6 Position the sprayed artificial flowers around the ring in an asymmetrical way. Wire stems can be pushed horizontally through the evergreens and into the wreath base. Tie two bows with the ribbon and neaten the ends by cutting them at a slant. Push half a stub wire through the loop at the back of each bow and insert into the wreath form.

7 Hang the wreath where it will catch flattering shafts of light to emphasize the gilding. To give your Christmas decorations a coordinated look, you could compose a smaller version of the wreath for a table decoration.

CHRISTMAS GREETINGS

You Will Need

selection of evergreens such as blue pine, ivy, cypress, and yew ● *dried grasses* ● *wheat* ● *gold spray paint* ● *roll of florists' silver wire* ● *4cm- (1½in-) wide decorative ribbon*

Welcome callers with a simple evergreen door posy, or make several to decorate the house during the festive season.

1 Cover the work surface with newspaper and spray a few heads of wheat and some trails of ivy with gold paint. Turn the materials over and spray them on the other side. Leave them to dry. Gather the wheat in a bunch of uneven lengths and bind the stems with silver wire. Tie the grass stems into a bunch and wire them.

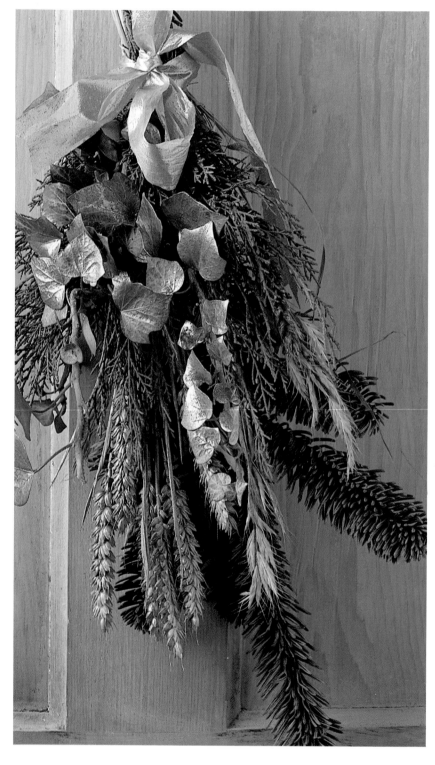

2 Place the largest component, the blue pine, on the table and arrange the other materials over it. Rearrange them until they form a pleasing shape. Bind all the stems together with silver wire. Tie the ribbon around the stems, tie into a bow and trim the ends by cutting at a slant.

TARTAN TRIO

You Will Need

plain white candles; these are 30cm (12 in) long ● snippings of evergreens such as blue pine, cypress, holly, yew, and box ● artificial holly berries ● seedheads, sprayed with gold paint ● secateurs (pruning shears) ● roll of florists' silver wire ● florists' scissors ● 4cm- (1½ in-) wide and 2.5cm- (1in-) wide ribbons ● scissors

Give plain white candles a festive look with bright trimmings of evergreens, berries, and ribbons. You can use them to decorate a window, a mantelpiece, or the dining table.

1 Cut short lengths of mixed evergreens and seedheads. Place a few stems against a candle and bind in place with silver wire. Add more stems, and bind in place around the candle until it is decorated with a ring of evergreens. Secure the binding wire. Hook the wires of the berry decorations over the silver wire. Tie a ribbon around the candle to conceal the wire, tie it in a bow and trim the ends.

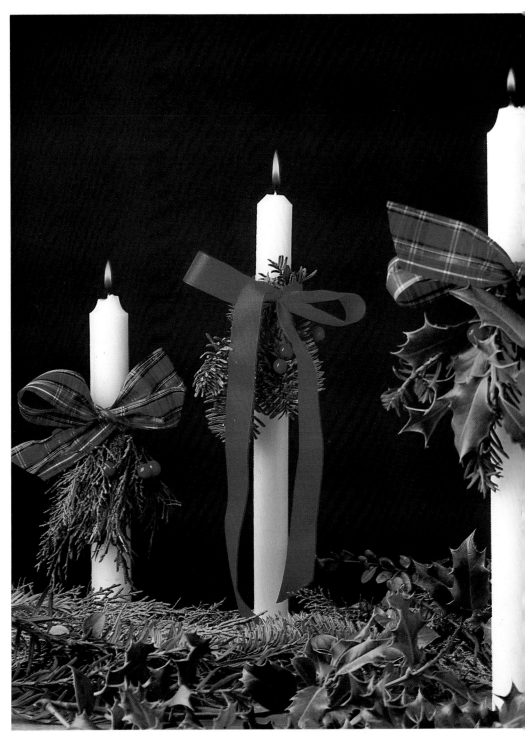

2 Display the candles among cuttings of evergreens. Do not leave lighted candles unattended.

WEDDING CELEBRATION

You Will Need

*pedestal-type fruit bowl or container
• piece of plastic-covered wire
mesh netting • narrow florists'
adhesive tape • scissors • selection
of flowers such as lilies, roses,
Singapore orchids, mimosa, spray
chrysanthemums, and
chincherinchee • sprays of
variegated foliage • florists' scissors*

Triumphant white lilies, delicate cream roses, exotic Singapore orchids, palest yellow mimosa – they all combine in an arrangement to capture the attention of the most starry-eyed bride. When the toasts are proposed, glasses are sure to be raised to the 'friend who did the flowers'.

1 Make your choice of flowers to complement the colour scheme chosen by the bride. This selection, in white, cream, and yellow, was chosen to add a hint of warmth to a winter-white scheme. Use a piece of wire mesh netting wide enough to fill the bowl. Hold it firmly in place with two criss-crossing strips of adhesive tape threaded through the wires, and short lengths looped around the wire and stuck onto the container at intervals.

2 Arrange the mimosa sprays to fan out from all sides of the bowl. When mimosa is not in season, or if the yellow flowers do not suit the colour scheme, slender sprays of foliage can be used instead. Arrange short stems of variegated foliage all around the rim of the container.

3 Arrange the lilies at two levels, with the fully-opened flowers facing the front of the design. Turn the container around and arrange more lilies in a similar way on the other side. The arrangement must be equally attractive when viewed from all sides.

4 Arrange a cluster of roses at the heart of the design, where the soft pale cream petals will emphasize the pure whiteness of the lilies. Arrange more roses in a similar position on the reverse of the bowl, then position the orchids to form a point in the centre. Position a few stems of chincherinchee on either side of the orchids.

5 Flatter the exotic flowers still further by arranging the simple daisy shapes of spray chrysanthemums in clusters between them. Spray the flowers with a fine mist of cool water, and keep the arrangement in a cool, shady place until the festivities begin.

GOING FOR GOLD

You Will Need

large glass or gilded container
• florists' adhesive tape • scissors
• large plastic foam-holding
container • absorbent stem-holding
foam • knife • flowers such as
spray chrysanthemums, carnations,
spray carnations, and gypsophila
• foliage such as eucalyptus and
flowering shrub • wheat and
linseed (flaxseed) • dried
hydrangea head • secateurs
(pruning shears) • roll of florists'
silver wire or twine • non-toxic
gold spray paint • 7.5cm- (3in-)
wide gold tinsel ribbon (optional)

When there's a 50th wedding anniversary to celebrate; someone you know has just been awarded a gold medal or gold watch; or you just want to put on a glittering party – go for gold. Our arrangement features a plain glass vase which has been dazzlingly transformed for the occasion with a handful of chocolate wrappers and a few dabs of glue. It's an idea you can adapt to create a variety of kaleidoscopic effects, using multi-coloured wrappers or metallic papers in a random patchwork.

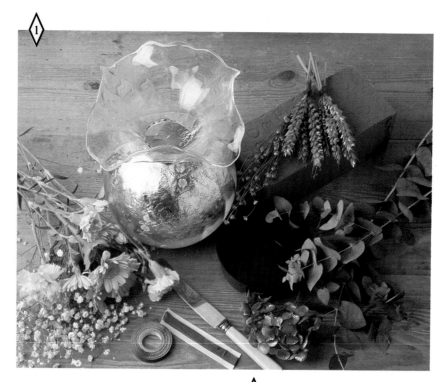

1 Cut short stems of wheat and linseed (flaxseed), group them into bunches and bind the stems with silver wire or twine. Cover a surface with newspaper and spray the wheat, linseed (flaxseed), and hydrangea with gold paint. Leave the materials to dry. The gold chocolate wrappings are stuck patchwork-fashion to the inside of the vase. A long-handled paintbrush is useful to manoeuvre and press them into place.

2 Shape the stem-holding foam to fit the plastic container by pressing the holder over the unsoaked block. Withdraw the container and cut around the imprint with a sharp knife. Soak the now circular piece of foam in water until it is saturated.

3 Cut two or three strips of adhesive clay, and press to the underside of the plastic holder. Press the holder onto the neck of the vase. Insert the soaked foam. (This vase had a raised rim which fitted closely around the plastic container, so it was not necessary to secure it further by taping over the foam with florists' adhesive tape). Create the outline of the arrangement with stems of eucalyptus, making a lop-sided triangle. Place other stems, and some sprays of flowering shrub, at the centre of the design.

◆4

4 Arrange the carnations to follow the overall outline of the design, then position the bunches of wheat and linseed (flaxseed) to fill the gaps. If the wheat stalks are too supple to push into the foam, it may be necessary to wrap a stub wire around the bunch and push one extended end into it.

◆5

5 Arrange the spray chrysanthemums around the design. If some of the sprays seem too dense, cut off one or two of the flowers and position the short stems at the front, where they will help to conceal the foam. Place the gold-sprayed hydrangea head in the centre, as a secondary and glittering focal point.

6 Position the spray carnations and cut off any small buds that interfere with the flow of the stems. Cut short sprays of gypsophila and place them around the base of the arrangement, where they will separate the golden-coloured flowers and create light spots. Tie a gold ribbon around the neck of the vase if desired.

PARTY PIECE

Flowers arranged for a buffet party or a special family celebration can use artistic licence in the matter of colour, break some of the rules, and earn nothing but praise. This party piece proves that you can blend red, blue, orange, mauve, yellow, and green – all the colours of the rainbow – in an arrangement that will command attention across a crowded room.

1 This is an occasion when you can give way to the temptation to choose several bunches of flowers of different types, colours, shapes, and sizes; when it is more important to match the mood of the occasion than the surrounding furnishings. Cut all the stem ends at a sharp angle, to facilitate the intake of water, and give the flowers a long drink in cool water before arranging them.

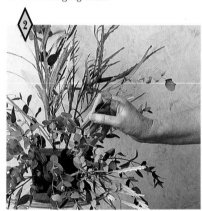

2 Stick a piece of adhesive clay to the underside of the plastic prong – some arrangers call it a 'frog's leg' – and press onto the container slightly behind the centre point. Press the soaked foam onto the spikes of the prong. Arrange the various types of foliage to make a fan shape across the centre of the arrangement, and to cascade down over the rim of the container at the front and sides.

3 Arrange the Peruvian lilies – here deep coral, peach, and cream colours were used – to follow the outline of the foliage. Cut some of the individual flowers on short stems and position them close to the foam.

4 Arrange the orchids in a triangular shape throughout the design, the tallest stem upright in the centre and progressively shorter stems slanted outwards at the front. If cutting the stems short involves cutting off some of the lower florets, position these as attractive 'fillers' close to the foam.

5 Arrange the irises to make a patch
of contrasting colour – the only
blue in the design – at the back. Cut
the stems at a sharply slanting angle.
The lower part of the stem and the
sword-like leaves can be used at the
reverse of the arrangement. Turn the
container around and fill in the back of
the design with sprays of foliage and a
selection of flowers to give the
arrangement depth and perspective.

6 Complete the arrangement by
adding the softening influence – as
far as the shape is concerned – of the
roses and carnations, which contrast
well with the principally trumpet- and
star-like shapes of the other flowers.
Add more foliage sprays to fill in any
gaps, and check that the design looks
equally good from either side.

A NOTE OF FORMALITY

When you are giving a formal dinner party – it may be for 'elder statesmen' in the family, business associates, or in celebration of an anniversary – the flower arrangements should set the tone of the occasion. This arrangement for the dining table is an all-round design in a silver-coloured urn, a profusion of flowers and foliage in white, cream, and silvery green.

1 Whether the dining table is set with crisp white linen or presents a highly polished surface; whether the china is ornately patterned or plain white – flowers in white, cream, and the palest of yellow compose a flatteringly pretty accessory.

3 Position the orchids to emphasize the central height, and fill in the middle ground with chincherinchee, Peruvian lilies, spray chrysanthemums, and roses.

2 Begin by building up the foundation of the design, the background of the mimosa, foliage, and hydrangea heads against which the more showy plant materials are seen. Arrange the mimosa sprays to form a fan shape on one side, tuck short clusters of hydrangea over the rim of the container, and position soft, silver-grey foliage such as ballota midway between them. Repeat the shape, if not the detail, on the other side.

4 Turn the container around and repeat the flower sequence on the other side, cutting the stems to achieve height balance.

5 Add short sprays of foliage to separate the flowers, so that each type can be seen to advantage. Turn the container around and check that the reverse is equally attractive. Add more flowers or foliage to correct any visual deficiencies.

BRIDESMAID'S HEADDRESS

You Will Need

stub wires • roll of florists' silver wire • white gutta percha (floral) tape • scissors • selection of flowers such as spray chrysanthemums, delphiniums, and roses • florists' scissors • 2.5cm- (1in-) wide patterned ribbon

A pretty circlet to be worn by a bridesmaid or a young bride at a summer wedding. The colours, a striking blend of apricot, cream, and blue, were chosen to complement the pale peach dresses of the young attendants in a country church.

1 To give the headdress more variety of colour, slender stems of dark blue larkspur and delphinium were blended with large florets, in a paler tint, cut from long spires of a similar plant. This also has the advantage of including flowers from a favourite garden without visibly denuding it.

2 You can make the base of the headdress from a piece of thick wire bound into a circle or, as was done here, use two stub wires twisted together to form a hoop. In either case, bind the wire with gutta percha (floral) tape, which is self-adhesive, taking it around the wire so that each strip overlaps the previous one.

3 Cut the flower stems to a length of about 4cm (1½in). Gather them into clusters of one or two spray chrysanthemums, a short spray of larkspur, and a delphinium floret. Bind the stems with a few twists of silver wire, and bind the cluster to the circle with the wire. Wire on a rose, more flower clusters, another rose and so on, until the floral circle is complete.

4 Tie the ribbon into a bow with long, trailing ends. Neaten the ends by cutting them at a slant. Thread the silver wire through the back of the ribbon loop and bind the bow to the headdress. Spray the flowers with a fine mist of cool water, and keep the decoration in a cool place – even in the refrigerator – until moments before setting off for the ceremony.

5 If the headdress is to be carried on a journey, wrap it carefully, perhaps in tissue paper in a box. Do not leave it in the full glare of the sun on the back seat of a car. A corsage, to be worn by a principal wedding guest, may be composed of similar flowers.

TABLE GARLAND

A garland is a lovely way to decorate a wedding or christening reception, a birthday, or other celebration. The garland, composed of long leafy stems, can be made to loop across the front of the buffet table, to encircle the rim of a table displaying the cake, or to drape on all four sides of a free-standing table.

1 Smilax, with its pliable stem and mass of bright green leaves forms a natural garland, and makes an attractive instant decoration, even without the addition of flowers. It is usually sold to order in bundles of five stems. Keep the stem ends in water until just before you assemble the garland, and the foliage should stay fresh for several days.

2 It saves time just before the event if the posies are made up in advance. Choose materials which will contrast well with the bright but delicate foliage of the garland. Cut the flower stems short, using five or six pieces of gypsophila, two small snippings of mimosa, and one or two spray chrysanthemums, according to their size. Gather the stems together and bind them with silver roll wire.

3 The posies can be spaced as close together or as wide apart as desired. As a general rule, the smaller the table the smaller the gap should be between the flowers.

Once the posies are assembled they can be placed in a shallow bowl of water before being attached to the garland.

4 Measure the length of garland needed for the side drapes and mark the centre. With the stems of the first posy towards the end of one of the lengths of foliage, bind the posy to the main stem with roll wire. Bind on more posies in the same way, reversing the direction of the stems when you reach the centre of the draped garland. Repeat the decoration with the remaining lengths of garland, but without reversing the direction of the flowers of the side trails.

5 Pin the garland to the cloth, adjusting the fall of the drape so that it is equal on all sides, and pin on the side trails. Check that the garland hangs well. Sometimes the weight of the posies will cause it to twist, with the flowers facing inwards. If this happens, pin the garland to the cloth at intervals. Pin ribbon or bows to the corners and the centre of the drapes.

WEDDING DECORATION

You Will Need

*plastic foam-holding tray, with
handle (available from florists)
● absorbent stem-holding foam,
soaked in water ● narrow florists'
adhesive tape (optional) ● selection
of flowers such as Peruvian lilies,
carnations, spray carnations, and
irises ● selection of slender foliage
such as broom and sprays of
variegated leaves and flowering
shrub ● florists' scissors ● 6mm-
(¼in-) wide ribbon ● stub wires
● wire cutters ● 2.5cm- (1in-)
wide ribbon ● wire or twine
for hanging*

Hanging decorations in a church or chapel complement the larger arrangements, the pedestal and windowsill designs, and further enhance the setting for a wedding or baptism. Such decorations may hang on the ends of pews, or on pillars, posts, and altar screens.

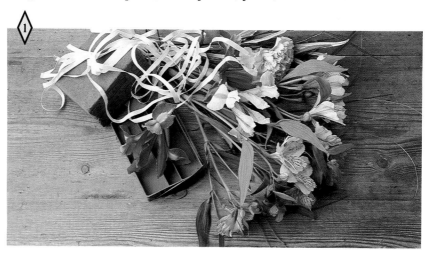

1 Before planning the wall decorations, take note of the background colour, whether it is dark oak or light pine, a relatively plain surface or a heavily-grained wood that is seen as a distinct pattern. Then choose the flower and foliage colours accordingly. If, for example, the theme of the wedding calls for flowers in pale colours, and the background wood is honey-coloured pine, give the design a clear, if wayward outline with dark foliage, and include some darker flowers to avoid a faded look. If making more than one decoration, divide the flowers and foliage into groups so that each matches the other.

2 Press a slice cut from a block of soaked foam into the plastic holder. Holding the container vertically, check that the foam is held firmly in place; it should be, because such holders are purpose-made for the size of the foam block. If it does not seem secure, tape the foam in place with two strips of florists' adhesive tape. Arrange long stems of slender foliage at the top and bottom of the holder and shorter sprays in the centre.

3 Cut short a carnation stem and position it just above the centre of the foam. Arrange the irises above and below it. Cut individual Peruvian lily flowers and arrange them to form the background of the design.

4 Arrange short sprays of foliage and flowering shrub to isolate some of the flowers and avoid a crowded look.

5 Extend the outline of the design with spray carnations. Cut the narrow ribbon into three lengths, double each one, and tie into a bow. Thread half a stub wire through the back of the loop, twist the ends, and press into the foam. Fold two or three lengths of wide ribbon in half, twist half a stub wire around the centre, twist the ends, and push them into the foam at the base of the decoration. Hang the decoration by threading a wire or length of twine through the hole in the handle. Spray the flowers with a fine mist of cool water, and keep them in a cool, shady place until needed.

FIT FOR A BRIDE

You Will Need

stub wires • wire cutters • roll of florists' silver wire • white gutta percha (floral) tape • scissors • selection of flowers such as Singapore orchids, Peruvian lilies, chincherinchee, irises, narcissus, mimosa, and freesias • florists' scissors • 4cm- (1½in-) wide satin ribbon • selection of foliage such as ballota and pampas grass

For a close friend or a relative of the bride it is both a pleasure and a privilege to compose the wedding bouquet. Confirm her preference for flower types and colours, then follow our easy step-by-step instructions for a bouquet fit for the most discerning bride.

1 Design the bride's bouquet to feature the flowers and colours that will set the scene for the ceremony and the reception and complement the colours she and her attendants will wear. If the bride's dress is in off-white or cream, avoid using pure-white flowers which would be unflattering to the fabric. Give all the flowers a long drink of cool water in a shady place before composing the bouquet.

2 It is essential to wire flowers for a bouquet of this kind, otherwise the bundle of stems forming the handle would both look and feel clumsy. Cut short the flower stems and push a stub wire into the ends. Bind over the join and down along the wire with overlapping gutta percha (floral) tape.

3 Gather together all the flowers that will form the centre of the bouquet – orchids, Peruvian lilies, freesias, and a rose – and bind the false wire stems with silver wire.

104

4 Hold the core of the bouquet in one hand and arrange slender stems of foliage to cascade over the flowers. Arrange a second layer of flowers around the front and sides of the central ones and bind all the stems and false stems with silver wire.

5 Arrange a third layer of flowers around the front and sides of the bouquet, bind the stems with silver wire, and add a few feature flowers close to the grip. Roses and short sprays of mimosa look attractive in this position. Bind the stems again with silver wire, and then with the satin ribbon, tying it just under the lowest of the flowers. Tie the ribbon in a bow and leave long, trailing ends. Spray the flowers with a fine mist of cool water, and keep in a cool place – even the refrigerator – until the ceremony is imminent.

BRIDAL POSY

You Will Need

*florists' scissors • roll of florists'
silver wire • a selection of flowers
such as roses, delphinium, freesias,
and spray carnations
• 4cm- (1½in-) wide velvet ribbon
• scissors*

Delicate and pretty summer flowers are arranged in colourful rings for a bridesmaid's posy that owes more than a little to Victorian styles. It is a design that would find favour with young brides, too, and is traditional enough to fulfil the requirement for 'something old' while comprising richly-coloured delphinium to provide 'something blue'.

1 If desired, the flower stems may be cut short, mounted on wires and bound with gutta percha (floral) tape before creating the bridal posy. In this design, which is seen as an informal posy and not a bouquet, the flowers are simply gathered together as a bunch. Give the flowers and foliage a long drink in cool water in a shady place before arranging them, since they will have no moisture source.

2 Gather the delphinium stems into a bunch and bind – not too tightly – with silver wire. Cut off any leaves that look out of place and obscure the flowers.

3 Holding the delphinium bunch in one hand, arrange first the freesias and then the spray carnations in graded layers around them. Rearrange the stems until the flower heads appear in neat rings. Bind the stems loosely with silver wire.

4 Arrange the ring of roses above the delphinium, where the delicate round flowers will contrast prettily with the dark spires. Arrange a few dainty sprays of foliage such as eucalyptus among the flowers, and position a rose beneath the ring of spray carnations. Rearrange the stems until the flowers rest in a pleasing sequence, then bind the stems with silver wire. If you make the posy a day before the wedding, leave it in water overnight before covering the stems with ribbon.

5 Wrap one end of the ribbon around the stems immediately beneath the rose and make a knot to secure it. Bind the stems with the ribbon and finish with a bow. Spray the flowers with a fine mist of cool water, avoiding the ribbon, and keep the posy in a cool place, perhaps in the refrigerator, until it is needed.

PASTEL TINTS

You Will Need

preformed absorbent foam ring, soaked in water; the one used here is 25cm (10in) diameter ● selection of flowers such as sweet peas, roses, spray carnations, Peruvian lilies, and gypsophila ● evergreen foliage such as ivy ● florists' scissors

A circlet of summer's palest and prettiest flowers – sweet peas, roses, carnations, and more – makes a delightful decoration for a garden party or an outdoor reception. To set the scene for a country wedding you could make these rings to match the bridal headdresses.

1 Short sprays and snippings of flowers can be used in this design, perhaps stems left over after composing larger arrangements for the occasion. Arrange a ring of ivy leaves around the inside and outside of the ring form to frame the flowers. Cut each sweet pea flower on a short stem and arrange them at intervals around the ring.

2 Complete the ring of sweet peas and arrange more ivy leaves between the flowers, to give the design a natural and countrified look.

3 Cut individual flowers of roses, Peruvian lilies and spray carnations and arrange them between the sweet peas. Some of the flowers should be placed around the inside and outside rims of the ring form. Cut short sprays of gypsophila and arrange them all around the ring. These diminutive white flowers have a soft veil-like effect and give the design a pretty look of informality.

4 A floral circlet can decorate a table top, a low shelf – where it may be seen against a stretch of green lawn – or a buffet table, where it would make an unusual centre-piece.

BIRTHDAY BASKET

You Will Need

flat rectangular basket • plastic prong • florists' adhesive clay • dry stem-holding foam • scissors • florists' scissors • selection of dried flowers such as larkspur, strawflowers, sea lavender, peonies, statice, and rosebuds • bundle of wheat stalks • 2.5cm- (1in-) wide satin ribbon • half a stub wire

A 'posy' of dried flowers makes a thoughtful and long-lasting gift for a birthday, anniversary, or other celebration. It is a design with an illusory secret – which is revealed in the step-by-step photographs.

1 Choose a basket with a rugged texture, which contrasts well with the delicacy of the flowers and serves as an effective frame. The flowers range from deep pink through coral and pale mauve to dark blue.

2 Fix the plastic prong with a strip of clay, just off-centre in the base of the basket and press a piece of dry foam onto it. Cut short lengths of spiky flowers – blue larkspur, for example – and position to make a fan shape.

3 Complete the outline of larkspur, then fill in the shape with short stems of statice and rosebuds. Begin a row of strawflowers to give more visual weight close to the centre.

4 Cut short stems of three peonies – this design features two in deep pink with a central flower in pale pink. Place them close to the edge of the foam to help to conceal it.

5 Now comes the illusion. Cut the wheat stalks in a range of lengths so that some will extend just beyond the rim of the basket and others will fall somewhat shorter. Push the stalks into the foam so that they form a broad, thick fan shape.

6 Fill in the floral posy with sprigs of sea lavender to soften the outline and extend beyond the basket rim. Tie a bow with the ribbon, trim the ends at a slant and push the stub wire through the back of the loop. Bend the wire into a U-shape and press it into the foam between the peonies. Fill in any gaps with more sea lavender.

TOOLS AND MATERIALS

~

This section is a quick and handy reference guide to all the equipment needed for successful arrangements – the best holding and fixing materials for the job, the correct equipment for preparing flowers and foliage prior to arranging, and the many ways of renovating and adapting containers for the occasion. Advice on compiling your own flower arranging tool kit will ensure you have everything to hand before you start, enabling you to get down to the more pleasant task of creating arrangements. Lastly, tips on selecting and harvesting plant materials will help to keep your arrangements in top condition, so all your efforts may be enjoyed for as long as possible.

Tools of the trade

Initially, you may find simple arrangements can be held in place in a narrow-necked container, without the need for additional 'mechanics' or fixing materials. As your interest in floral art develops however, and you want to compose arrangements with specific shapes, place stems at wayward angles, and adapt containers for all types of floral use, you will find a selection of water-holding and stem-holding materials especially useful. You will also want to build your own tool kit of other specialized equipment, which will make the task of preparing containers and harvesting and preparing plant materials both quicker and easier.

Stem-holding materials

There are three principal means of holding stems in place in arrangements of fresh flowers and foliage: the use of crumpled wire netting, absorbent polystyrene foam, and metal pinholders. Other methods, such as pushing stems into a handful of pebbles in a decorative glass vase, have a more limited application.

The first of these materials, wire netting, is used to tame stems arranged in wide-necked containers such as large jugs or bowls and baskets fitted with an inner water-holding liner. You can buy plastic-covered netting with a 2.5cm (1in) mesh, of the kind shown in many of

*Useful tools from left to right:
Selection of pinholders, florists'
scissors, absorbent stem-
holding foam, sharp knives,
florists' adhesive clay, narrow
florists' adhesive tape, scissors,
secateurs (pruning shears),
plastic saucer, candle cup, and
wire mesh netting.* **Above**

FIXING FLORISTS' WIRE
MESH NETTING

You Will Need

*container with a large
aperture* ● *piece of
plastic-covered florists'
wire mesh netting* ● *wire
cutters* ● *narrow florists'
adhesive tape* ● *scissors*

Preparing a container in this way will help you to
anchor stems of fresh or dried flowers in a casual
and informal design.

*Crumple the wire netting into a ball and place it in
the neck of the container. If you wish to position
some of the stems to slant at a low angle, ease the
wire so that it forms a mound extending slightly
above the level of the container rim. Remember
that the lowest of the plant materials will have to be
positioned so that they conceal this holding
material.*

*Cut two lengths of tape slightly longer than the
diameter of the container opening. Thread the first
strip under the wire in two places, take it across the
container, and stick it to the rim on each side.
Cross the second strip at right angles to the first
and fix it in the same way. Threading the tape
under the wire ensures that the ball of wire does
not slip down into the container.*

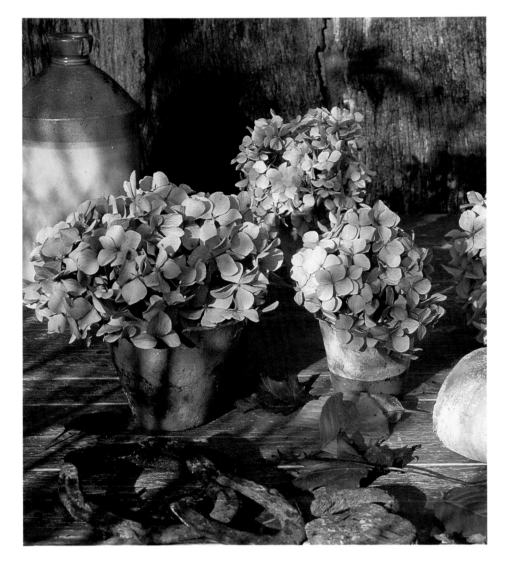

As informal as can be – a collection of earthenware flowerpots topped by greeny-blue hydrangea heads could decorate the table for an outdoor buffet or barbecue, or a supper party in a farmhouse-style kitchen. **Left**

Cut out for a conservatory – this open-work vase is fitted with a plastic saucer of soaked foam to support a colourful cascade of godetia and sweet peas. **Opposite**

the project photographs, or use the type sold in garden centres for outdoor use. A piece of netting measuring about 24cm × 34cm (9in × 13in) is enough for most average-size containers, with proportionately smaller or larger pieces for other container types.

Crush the netting lightly in your hands to form it into a ball and push it into the neck of the container. If you are using uncovered netting, which will have a tangle of rough edges, in a precious container such as one made of silver or glass, take the precaution of first lining the inner rim with a protective layer of insulating tape.

Although the ball of wire should fit tightly into the container opening, it is advisable to secure it, to prevent it slipping or becoming lop-sided as you position the stems. To do this, use narrow florists' adhesive tape, which is sold in several colours – green, white, and brown

among them. When the lower flowers and leaves in a design will dip and trail low over the container rim and conceal the fixings, you can criss-cross two lengths of holding tape over the wire and down about 2cm (¾in) over the rim. When the rim will not be covered with plant materials in this way, and the tape might show, cut several short lengths, wrap each one around a piece of wire, and twist it inwards, to stick to the inside of the container. When you dismantle an arrangement, you can straighten out the wire and store it for future use.

The use of crumpled wire netting makes it possible to arrange, for example, three stems of Madonna lilies in a wide-necked vase, each stem facing in the direction you have determined. However, when you want the outline to be more adventurous, or more deliberately wayward, or if you want to position some stems horizontally or at a steep

downward angle, your choice of stem-holding material will be absorbent polystyrene foam. This material, which is sold under several brand names and is usually dull green, has had the most far-reaching and significant effect on the art of flower arranging, and has made possible shapes and outlines that could not otherwise have been achieved. The foam is sold in two main sizes: in 6cm (2½in) deep cylinders with an 8cm (3in) diameter, and in blocks measuring 22.5cm × 11cm × 7.5cm (9in × 4¼in × 3in), which you can cut to any size and shape.

Florists sell inexpensive plastic saucers, usually green or white, which have an indent just the right size to hold one of the foam cylinders, and plastic 'candle cups', made with a cork-shaped plug that fits into the top of a candlestick. In this way, with a cylinder of stem-holding foam secured in a water-holding dish, you can convert a tall container or a household item, be it a wine carafe, decorative tin, or slender vase, into an improvised pedestal, and arrange arching stems to cascade attractively, dipping far below the rim.

The taller the converted container, the more precarious the foam holder may be. To attach a plastic saucer to the top of a tall vase, and hold the soaked foam securely in place, use a strip of florists' adhesive clay. This is another product sold under many trade names and which may be either brown or green. Press the clay around the rim of the

FIXING A SAUCER OF STEM-HOLDING FOAM

By preparing a container in this way you can use a tall vase, carafe, or jug as a pedestal, positioning flower and foliage stems to slant both downwards and horizontally.

1 Cut small lengths of adhesive clay and press them onto the underside of the plastic saucer, where it will come into contact with the top of the container. Press the saucer firmly in place to hold it securely.

You Will Need

tall container ● strip of florists' adhesive clay ● plastic foam-holding saucer, or you could use an upturned coffee jar lid ● cylinder of stem-holding foam, absorbent or dry according to the materials to be arranged ● narrow florists' adhesive tape ● scissors

A highly-polished brass candlestick becomes a pedestal container when it is fitted with a plastic saucer and a cylinder of soaked foam. The dome of cypress and ivy leaves forms a foundation for a casual placement of freesias and tulips. **Right**

2 Soak the foam if it is to hold fresh flowers and foliage. Press the foam cylinder into the indent in the saucer. Cut two lengths of adhesive tape long enough to go over the foam, across the saucer and down onto the container rim. Stick them in place, criss-crossing them on top of the foam.

container or saucer, and press the saucer firmly in place. Insert the cylinder of soaked foam and criss-cross two strips of narrow florists' adhesive tape over it, down over the rim of the saucer and, for extra security, onto the container. If the flower arrangement thus elevated is to be composed of heavy materials, such as substantial stems of foliage or shrubs, it is advisable to weight the container first with ballast. A glass container will need presentable materials such as glass marbles, coloured pebbles, or coloured sand; others can be held steady with a few handfuls of sand, soil, or gravel.

Absorbent foam blocks have many applications in flower arrangements, ranging from massive to miniature. You may need to use a block standing on end for a tall arrangement in a deep basket, or two blocks side-by-side for a larger design. Cut strips to fit inside square or rectangular containers or to wedge in the neck of other shapes, or use a cube of the material in a dish to create an L-shaped design in light or middleweight materials.

Cut the foam when it is dry, and keep the off-cuts, however small, to use at other times. You may, for example, want to pack a wide container with crushed and soaked foam, a method of anchoring stems that may be used when a mound of crumpled wire netting or a protruding block of foam could not be concealed by the plant materials. Whenever you want to position stems to slant downwards or lie horizontally, cut the foam so it extends about 2.5cm (1in) above the rim of the container;

it is this extra height that allows them to do so. Shape the foam so that there will be enough space around it to top up the container with water and keep the material permanently moist.

Soak the foam in a bowl of cold water until it has absorbed its capacity – this will take about 20 minutes. Once it is in place in an arrangement, top it up with water every day and, when the design is dismantled, store the foam in a plastic bag or box until you want to use it again. If you allow it to dry out, it will not reabsorb moisture.

The third principal means of anchoring stems is by using a pinholder, a flat heavy weight sold in a range of sizes and a variety of shapes, and which has a series of vertical pins arranged close together in straight rows. A pinholder may be used in the base of a deep container to anchor long or especially heavy stems, whether or not crumpled netting is used at the neck; and in flat dishes when, for example, an L-shaped design is created. Stems may in this case be pushed both vertically and horizontally between the spikes and the stem ends covered with water. Fix the pinholders to the base of a dry container with a few dabs of florists' adhesive clay, and conceal them, in shallow containers, with granite chippings, small pebbles or broken glass.

Tool kit

Beyond the stem-holding materials and the means of fixing them, there are a few items that are useful in the care and preparation of plant materials.

- A good-quality pair of secateurs or pruning shears are a 'must' for cutting branches and other woody stems. Dry the secateurs after use, and keep them in a dry place.
- Florists' scissors are useful for cutting less substantial flower and foliage stems, both in the garden and at the work table.
- A craft knife with a short, sharp blade is useful for scraping the bark from woody stems and splitting the stem ends, both ways of enabling the plant material to take up moisture.
- A watering-can with a thin spout is useful for topping up containers with water and is more efficient than a jug, which may cause spills and surface damage.
- A water spray or plant mister that emits a fine, even mist is invaluable for spraying fresh flower arrangements before you place them in position, and for giving them frequent cooling-down showers, especially in hot weather. Remember to remove arrangements to a water-resistant surface before spraying them.

In summer a large, open fireplace becomes a stage for an ever-changing floral display. The willow basket, lined with a deep bowl and two blocks of soaked foam, holds a countrified arrangement of wild flowers – daisy-like marguerites, campion, and buttercups. **Opposite**

A bright spot of colour anywhere you may need it in the garden, on the patio or balcony – a wooden garden basket arranged with a towering asymmetrical display of cereals, grasses, dahlias, and chrysanthemums in vibrant and harmonizing colours. **Below**

HARVESTING AND SELECTING FLOWERS

No matter how casual or carefully calculated an arrangement may be, no matter what, if any, holding material is used, one consideration is paramount: all the plant material in the display, every flower and leaf, seedhead and berry must be in perfect condition. This means you must harvest materials from the garden or countryside when they are in the peak of condition, and be critically selective whenever you purchase flowers from a florist or market stall.

In general, it is best to leave flowers to reach a mid-way stage of maturity on the plant. Cut rosebuds and carnations as they are just beginning to unfurl, and when tall spires – including larkspur, delphinium, gladioli, Canterbury bells, and orchids – are showing the full beauty of only the lower florets. Other florets will be at various stages of development all the way up the stem to the tightly-closed top-most buds, which are suitable candidates for use as 'points' in geometric designs. At this stage, plant materials are advanced enough to survive without further nutrition from the plant, and will give you the joy of watching them unfold day by day. Of course, there will be times when you will want to gather a handful of fully-opened roses with each delicate petal spread out, or a bunch of papery poppies to put on the kitchen table. Theirs will be a short vase-life, but a beautiful one.

It is important to plan your harvesting time with something of the precision of a farmer garnering his crops. Avoid cutting flowers and foliage in the heat of the sun, when they are at their most vulnerable and least able to recover from the transition from growing plant to design component. In any case, especially in hot weather, it is best to put stems straight into water as soon as they are cut. For large stems – an armful of dahlias or branches of privet – this may mean taking a bucket of cool water from patch to patch. For smaller materials – a handful of marigolds or a few stems of freesia – you can simply carry a bowl of water in the basket over your arm.

Whether they are the fruits of your own harvest or a selective purchase, treat flower and foliage stems carefully as soon as you bring them indoors, using a simple process known as 'conditioning'. Strip off any leaves that would come below the water line, since these would sour the water and shorten the vase-life of the material. Using sharp secateurs (pruning shears) or florists' scissors, recut the stem ends at a sharp angle, to allow the largest possible area to soak up moisture. In the case of hollow and fleshy stems such as daffodil and delphinium, do this

under water, the stems held just below the water line in a bowl. This extra precaution helps prevent the formation of air locks, which inhibit moisture intake and, again, shorten the vase-life of the flowers.

Stand all the stems in cool – not ice-cold – water for at least a couple of hours, longer if possible. Wrap bunches of flowers such as tulips and ranunculus, which have a bad reputation for drooping, in newspaper, and stand them up to their necks – but not over the flower heads – in water.

Once the plant material has had a long, reviving drink, take a critical look at each stem. Snip off damaged leaves, and remove all the leaves from flowers such as spray chrysanthemums, which do not have the staying

Completely at home in its surroundings, the small pottery basket is arranged with buttercups and daisies and a single marguerite – a daisy look-alike on a larger scale. The design would also look at home in a young child's room. **Opposite**

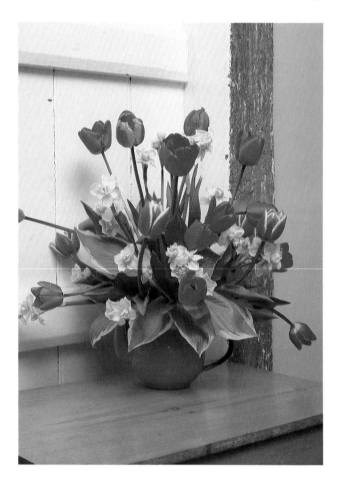

Tulips can have a wayward look. Use this to advantage by positioning the stems to curve in different directions, while composing a well-ordered cluster of leaves and flowers at the heart of the design. **Above**

power of the blooms. Examine each flower carefully, and gently pick off any damaged outer petals – those of roses, for instance – which spoil the beauty of an otherwise perfect specimen.

Heat and light are significant factors in the development and longevity of the cut stems, just as they are when plants are growing. If you want to hold back the development of cut flowers – say, for a party two or three days ahead – keep them in water in a cool, dark place or even, where small quantities are concerned, in the refrigerator. If, on the other hand, you are impatient for flowers to open more readily stand them in warm water, in a warm place for a few hours.

The twin elements, heat and light, have equally significant effects on the lasting qualities of a completed arrangement. It is important to spray fresh flowers with a fine mist of cool water at least once a day and more frequently in hot weather, and to shelter them from direct heat or sunlight. No matter how tempting it may be to place an arrangement of fresh or dried flowers where it will be lit by the full force of the summer sun, don't do it; or, at least, not for long. Position it in a sheltered spot, beside the window but not facing it, or on a table, desk, chair or stool – anything but a shelf over a radiator.

Gradually the flowers will fade. Postpone this process for as long as possible by removing them from the container and recutting the stem ends, and giving them fresh water every day. Discard some short-lived species, and replace them with others; a fresh bunch of paper-white narcissus set among a bevy of lilies, tulips, and spray carnations will help to rejuvenate the arrangement's decorative potential.

INDEX

Step-by-step projects are written in *italic*.

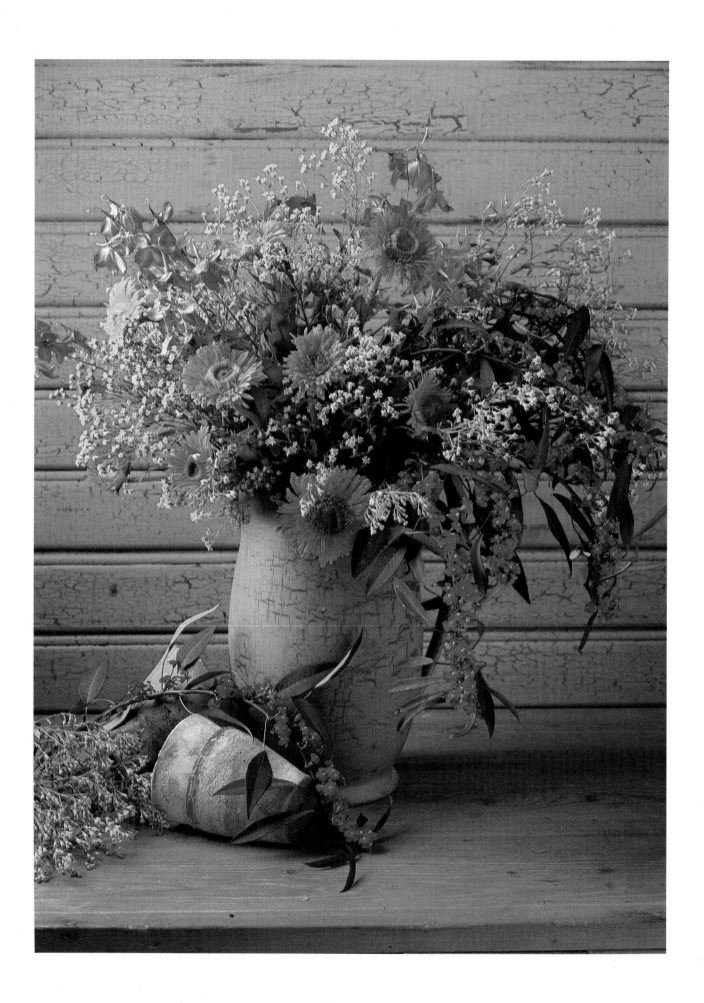